Bookkeeping and Accounting Test for International Communication

BATIC
（国際会計検定）®

公式問題集

発行所／東京商工会議所
発売元／中央経済社

本書の特徴と使い方

　この本は、東京商工会議所が主催する「BATIC（国際会計検定）®」対策の問題集です。

　本書は「問題編」と「解答編」で構成されており、各 Chapter の内容は「BATIC 公式テキスト」に対応しています。また、最後の「総合練習問題」は、実際の試験問題を想定して作られています。

　問題編は選択式の問題と記述式の問題で構成されています。

　解答編では解答の他、和訳と簡単な解説がついていますので、単に正解の確認にとどまらず、理解を深めてください。

BATIC （国際会計検定）®
Bookkeeping & Accounting Test For International Communication

■試験要項

主催	東京商工会議所・各地商工会議所
出題範囲	公式テキストの基礎知識とそれを理解した上での応用力を問います。
合否の基準	400点満点・スコア制
スコアと称号	得点に応じて称号が付与されます。 ・初級レベル（50%）……Entry ・中級レベル（80%）……Middle ・上級レベル（90%）……Advanced
受験料（税込）	5,500円

試験方式	IBT	CBT
概要	受験者ご自身のパソコン・インターネット環境を利用し、受験いただく試験方式です。 受験日時は所定の試験期間・開始時間から選んでお申込みいただきます。	各地のテストセンターにお越しいただき、備え付けのパソコンで受験いただく試験方式です。 受験日時は所定の試験期間・開始時間から選んでお申込みいただきます。 ※受験料の他にCBT利用料2,200円（税込）が別途発生します。
試験期間	※IBT・CBT方式共通 ■第43回　【申込期間】　6月15日（水）〜　6月24日（金） 　　　　　【試験期間】　7月22日（金）〜　8月 8日（月） ■第44回　【申込期間】　10月 5日（水）〜10月14日（金） 　　　　　【試験期間】　11月11日（金）〜11月28日（月）	
申込方法	インターネット受付のみ ※申込時にはメールアドレスが必要です。	
試験時間	70分 ※別に試験開始前に本人確認、受験環境の確認等を行います。	
受験場所	自宅や会社等 （必要な機材含め、受験者ご自身でご手配いただく必要があります）	全国各地のテストセンター

※BATIC（国際会計検定）®は、2022年度の実施を持ちまして終了させていただくことになりました。予めご了承ください。

お問合せ
東京商工会議所検定センター
TEL：03-3989-0777（土日・祝日・年末年始を除く　10：00〜18：00） https://kentei.tokyo-cci.or.jp/

■試験範囲

Basic Concepts of Accounting and Bookkeeping	会計と簿記の基本概念
Transactions and Journal Entries	取引と仕訳
Journal and Ledger	仕訳帳と元帳
Trial Balance	試算表
Adjusting Entries	決算修正仕訳
Accounting for Inventory and Cost of Sales	棚卸資産と売上原価の会計処理
Worksheet and Closing Entries	精算表と締切仕訳
Financial Statements	財務諸表
Basic Assumptions and GAAP	基本的な前提と GAAP
Financial Statement Analysis	財務諸表分析
Internal Control	内部統制
Cash Control	現金管理
Accounting for Assets and Liabilities	資産と負債の会計処理

CONTENTS 〈目次〉

Contents

解答編

CHAPTER 1 ―簿記の基本概念―

1ヶ月目 2ヶ月目 3ヶ月目
難易度レベル ★ ☆ ☆

Basic Concepts of Bookkeeping

Bookkeeping & Accounting Test for International Communication

BATIC

1-1

Which of the following transactions reduces equity?

(1) Bought furniture on account.

(2) Received fees for services rendered.

(3) Bought stationery for cash that was recorded as asset.

(4) Bought stationery for cash that was recorded as expense.

(5) Borrowed $5,000 from a bank.

1-2

B. Wales began operation by investing cash into the firm. The effect of this transaction for the firm was to

(1) Increase an asset, increase a liability.

(2) Increase an asset, increase equity.

(3) Decrease an asset, increase equity.

(4) Increase an asset, decrease a liability.

(5) No effect

1-3

A Company bought machinery on account. The effect of this transaction was to

(1) Increase an asset, decrease another asset.

(2) Increase an asset, increase equity.

(3) Increase an asset, increase a liability.

(4) Decrease an asset, decrease a liability.

(5) Increase a liability, decrease equity.

1-4

B Company paid creditors for the balance. The effect of this transaction was to

(1) Increase an asset, increase a liability.
(2) Decrease an asset, decrease a liability.
(3) Decrease an asset, decrease equity.
(4) Increase an asset, decrease another asset.
(5) Decrease an asset, increase equity.

1-5

B Company purchased equipment for cash.
What is the net effect of this transaction on the amount of assets, liabilities and equity?

	Assets	Liabilities	Equity
(1)	Increase	No effect	Increase
(2)	Increase	Increase	No effect
(3)	Decrease	Decrease	No effect
(4)	Decrease	No effect	Decrease
(5)	No effect	No effect	No effect

1-6

Burr Company paid premium of $100 for a fire insurance policy.
Journalize this transaction.

Dr.
  Cr.

1-7

Suzuki began his business investing $5,000 in cash, $3,000 worth of supplies and equipment valued at $10,000, and a $5,000 note payable for the equipment. The equity of the business is

(1) $ 5,000.
(2) $13,000.
(3) $18,000.
(4) $23,000.
(5) None of the above

1-8

When total assets increased by €3,000 during the current fiscal year and equity also increased by €1,000 during the same fiscal year, the effect on the amount of total liabilities is a

(1) €2,000 increase.
(2) €4,000 increase.
(3) €3,000 decrease.
(4) €1,000 decrease.
(5) None of the above

1-9

Machinery in the amount of $7,000 was purchased for $4,000 in cash with the balance on account. Which of the following is the effect of this transaction on the accounting equation?

	Assets	Liabilities	Equity
(1)	+ 7,000	+ 3,000	− 4,000
(2)	+ 7,000	− 4,000 ; − 3,000	No effect
(3)	+ 4,000	− 4,000	No effect
(4)	+ 7,000 ; − 4,000	+ 3,000	No effect
(5)	None of the above		

1-10

Assume that C Company has assets of $300,000 and equity of $200,000. What is the amount of liabilities?

(1) $500,000

(2) $300,000

(3) $200,000

(4) $100,000

(5) None of the above

1-11

D Company had the following transactions during April. Which of the following T-accounts is the correct cash account of D?

   a. Mr. Y established D Company by investing $30,000 on 4/1.

   b. D Company paid rent expense for $10,000 on 4/10.

   c. D Company paid salary for $5,000 on 4/20.

(1)

Cash			
4/1	30,000		
4/10	10,000		
4/20	5,000		

(2)

Cash			
		4/1	30,000
		4/10	10,000
		4/20	5,000

(3)

Cash			
4/10	10,000	4/1	30,000
4/20	5,000		

(4)

Cash			
4/20	5,000	4/1	30,000
		4/10	10,000

(5)

Cash			
4/1	30,000	4/10	10,000
		4/20	5,000

1-12

Which of the following accounts is classified into assets?

(1) Cash

(2) Share capital

(3) Retained earnings

(4) Accounts payable

(5) Interest income

1-13

ABC Company has liabilities of $300,000 and equity of $180,000. What is the amount of ABC's assets?

(1) $120,000
(2) $150,000
(3) $180,000
(4) $300,000
(5) $480,000

1-14

Classify the following accounts into assets, liabilities, equity, income or expenses.

(1) Equipment
(2) Sales
(3) Salaries expense
(4) Accounts receivable
(5) Notes payable

1-15

Record the following transactions in T-accounts.

(a) Mr. Meyer invested €20,000 cash to start his own company that issued equivalent ordinary shares.

(b) ABC Company purchased equipment with €4,000 cash.

(c) XYZ Company paid €300 cash for utilities expense.

CHAPTER 2 —取引と仕訳—

難易度レベル ★ ☆ ☆

Transactions and Journal Entries

Bookkeeping & Accounting Test for International Communication

BATIC

2-1

Star Corporation paid travel expense of $200 to the travel agent. Which of the following journal entries is correct?

(1) Cash   200
        Travel expense   200
(2) Cash   200
        Rent expense   200
(3) Bonds payable   200
        Cash   200
(4) Travel expense   200
        Cash   200
(5) None of the above

2-2

Record each transaction in T-accounts below.

July   5   Paid €250 for rent for the month.
      14   Paid €3 for stationery for the office.
      19   Paid €2 for stamps.

2-3

Terry Corporation bought merchandise for $500 on account. Which of the following journal entries is correct?

(1) Purchases   500
      Accounts payable   500

(2) Cash   500
      Purchases   500

(3) Accounts receivable   500
      Cash   500

(4) Purchases   500
      Cash   500

(5) Accounts payable   500
      Purchases   500

2-4

Record the following transaction in the T-accounts below.

Feb. 3   Sold merchandise for $300 on account.

2-5

Record each transaction in T-accounts below.

Feb. 3   Sold R. Smith merchandise on account for $300.

 11   Received $100 cash from R. Smith.

 18   Received $200 cash in full from R. Smith.

2-6

A customer returned merchandise in the amount of €50 sold on account. Which of the following journal entries should the seller record in connection with this transaction? The seller adopted sales returns and allowances account for the returned goods.

(1) Sales	50	
Cash		50
(2) Sales returns and allowances	50	
Cash		50
(3) Sales	50	
Accounts receivable		50
(4) Sales returns and allowances	50	
Accounts receivable		50
(5) None of the above		

2-7

On February 5, C Company sold goods for $1,000 with discount terms of 2%, 10 days.

If the purchaser pays on February 6, how much should he/she pay?

(1) $1,000
(2) $ 980
(3) $ 998
(4) $ 20
(5) $0

2-8

On December 1, 20X0, Company A sold Company B goods for $1,000 with discount terms of 2%, 10 days. Company B paid the whole amount on December 12, 20X0. What amount should be discounted?

(1) $1,000
(2) $ 200
(3) $ 20
(4) $ 10
(5) $0

2-9

Norton Company borrowed money in the amount of $400 from a bank, giving notes in exchange.
Journalize this transaction.

    Dr.
        Cr.

2-10

Norton Company repaid €100 on the above notes payable. Journalize this transaction.

    Dr.
        Cr.

2-11

Below is an example of a note receivable.

November 1, 20X0

I promise to pay ABC Company $900, 20 days from November 1, 20X0, at 6% annual interest.

William Smith

Assume that 1 year = 360 days.
(a) Who is the maker of the note?
(b) Who is the payee of the note?
(c) What is the maturity date of the note?
(d) What is the maturity value of the note?

2-12

Kent Corporation received $5 interest for a loan of money. Journalize this transaction.

Dr.

Cr.

2-13

SSS Corporation issued a 90-day, 10% promissory note with a face value of $20,000 to a creditor in payment of accounts payable. Prepare journal entries to record (a) and (b). Assume that 1 year = 360 days.

(a) The issuance of the note
(b) The payment of the note, including appropriate interest

2-14

Record the following journal entries for A Company.

(a) Issued ordinary shares for invested $9,000 cash.
(b) Bought $5,000 worth of office furniture on account.
(c) Received $1,500 as interest income.
(d) Paid $8,000 for office equipment by cash.
(e) Paid salaries of $600 by cash.

2-15

Record the following journal entries for B Company.

(a) Invested $20,000 in cash, $1,500 in inventory, $10,000 in furniture, and $11,000 in equipment to begin its operations.

(b) Purchased supplies worth $2,000 on account.

(c) Billed fees for $3,000.

(d) Invested additional cash of $6,000.

(e) Paid half of accounts payable by cash.

2-16

A Company sold goods on account. Indicate the correct journal entry.

(1) Debit Sales, Credit Cash

(2) Debit Cash, Credit Sales

(3) Debit Sales, Credit Accounts receivable

(4) Debit Accounts receivable, Credit Sales

(5) None of the above

2-17

F Company paid employee's salary. Indicate the correct journal entry.

(1) Debit Cash, Credit Employee

(2) Debit Cash, Credit Salaries expense

(3) Debit Salaries expense, Credit Cash

(4) Debit Employee, Credit Cash

(5) None of the above

2-18

The account below indicates a transaction of ABC Company.

Choose the appropriate description.

Cash		Fees Income	
100			100

(1) Withdrew cash for personal use.

(2) Paid salaries.

(3) Borrowed money from a bank.

(4) Invested cash in the firm.

(5) None of the above

2-19

Compute the amount of net purchases based on the following information:

Purchases	$12,500
Freight on purchases	1,500
Purchase returns and allowances	2,100

2-20

ABC Company sold merchandise for €2,000 with the discount terms of 4%, 30 days on April 5. The purchaser paid on April 20. Which of the following journal entries should ABC make on April 20?

(1) Cash   80
    Sales   80

(2) Cash   80
    Sales discounts   80

(3) Cash   1,920
    Sales discounts   80
      Accounts receivable   2,000

(4) Sales   80
    Cash   80

(5) Sales discounts   80
    Accounts receivable   80

2-21

ABC Company bought merchandise of $1,000 with the discount terms of 3%, 20 days on April 5.

(a) If ABC pays on April 10, how much should it pay?

(1) $0
(2) $ 30
(3) $ 833
(4) $ 970
(5) $1,000

(b) If ABC pays on April 30, how much should it pay?

(1) $0
(2) $ 30
(3) $ 833
(4) $ 970
(5) $1,000

2-22

XYZ Company sold merchandise for $50,000 cash on October 1. Since the customer returned damaged merchandise, XYZ refunded $150 cash on October 20.

(a) Which of the following journal entries should XYZ Company make on October 1?

(1) Accounts receivable	50,000	
Sales		50,000
(2) Cash	50,000	
Accounts receivable		50,000
(3) Cash	50,000	
Sales		50,000
(4) Sales	50,000	
Accounts receivable		50,000
(5) Sales	50,000	
Cash		50,000

(b) Which of the following journal entries should XYZ Company make on October 20?

(1) Sales   150
        Accounts receivable   150

(2) Sales   150
        Sales returns and allowances   150

(3) Sales returns and allowances   150
        Accounts receivable   150

(4) Sales returns and allowances   150
        Cash   150

(5) Sales returns and allowances   150
        Sales   150

2-23

XYZ Company issued an interest-bearing note of €10,000, 30 days from the date, at face value in settlement of an account payable. The face rate of annual interest for the note was 9.0%.

(a) When XYZ Company issued the note, which of the following journal entries should it make?

(1) Accounts payable	10,000	
Notes payable		10,000
(2) Cash	10,000	
Notes payable		10,000
(3) Notes payable	10,000	
Accounts payable		10,000
(4) Notes receivable	10,000	
Accounts receivable		10,000
(5) Notes receivable	10,000	
Cash		10,000

(b) When XYZ Company settled the note, which of the following journal entries should it make? Assume that 1 year = 360 days.

(1) Cash   10,075

        Notes payable   10,000

        Interest expense   75

(2) Cash   10,900

        Notes payable   10,000

        Interest expense   900

(3) Notes payable   10,000

        Cash   10,000

(4) Notes payable   10,000

        Interest expense   75

        Cash   10,075

(5) Notes payable   10,000

        Interest expense   900

        Cash   10,900

CHAPTER 3 ―仕訳帳と元帳―

Journal and Ledger

Bookkeeping & Accounting Test for International Communication
BATIC

3-1

Journalize the following transactions and then post them to the ledger.

20X0

April	3	Bought €275 of merchandise on account.
	5	Sold €800 of merchandise for cash.
	10	Bought €320 of merchandise for cash.
	18	Sold €700 of merchandise on account.

General Journal — J3

Date	Account and Explanation	P.R.	Debit	Credit
20X0				

General Ledger

Cash — 101

Date	Explanation	P.R.	Debit	Credit	Balance
20X0					

Accounts Receivable — 102

Date	Explanation	P.R.	Debit	Credit	Balance
20X0					

Accounts Payable — 201

Date	Explanation	P.R.	Debit	Credit	Balance
20X0					

Sales — 401

Date	Explanation	P.R.	Debit	Credit	Balance
20X0					

Purchases — 501

Date	Explanation	P.R.	Debit	Credit	Balance
20X0					

3-2

ABC Company had the following transactions during May 20X0.

Date	Transaction
May 2	Issued €10,000 of ordinary shares for equivalent equipment.
6	Purchased €2,500 of merchandise on account.
10	Sold €3,000 of merchandise for cash.
14	Purchased €30 of office supplies for cash.
19	Sold €1,800 of merchandise on account.
22	Paid €2,000 cash for settlement of an account payable.
28	Received €600 cash for settlement of an account receivable.

Journalize and then post them to the ledger.

General Journal   J4

Date	Account and Explanation	P.R.	Debit	Credit
20X0				

General Ledger

Cash   101

Date	Explanation	P.R.	Debit	Credit	Balance
20X0					

Accounts Receivable   102

Date	Explanation	P.R.	Debit	Credit	Balance
20X0					

Equipment 110

Date	Explanation	P.R.	Debit	Credit	Balance
20X0					

Accounts Payable 201

Date	Explanation	P.R.	Debit	Credit	Balance
20X0					

Share Capital 301

Date	Explanation	P.R.	Debit	Credit	Balance
20X0					

Sales 401

Date	Explanation	P.R.	Debit	Credit	Balance
20X0					

Purchases 501

Date	Explanation	P.R.	Debit	Credit	Balance
20X0					

Office Supplies Expense 508

Date	Explanation	P.R.	Debit	Credit	Balance
20X0					

CHAPTER 4　—試算表—

1ヶ月目 2ヶ月目 3ヶ月目

難易度レベル ★ ☆ ☆

Trial Balance

Bookkeeping & Accounting Test for International Communication

BATIC

4-1

Which of the following errors would be detected by a trial balance?

(1) Failing to record the whole entry for a transaction.

(2) Journalizing one part of an entry or a different amount than the other part.

(3) Double journalizing or posting an entry twice.

(4) Posting to an improper account.

(5) All of the above

4-2

ABC Company's trial balance is as follows. Since some accounts have been presented improperly from the ledger to the trial balance, it does not balance.

Correct the trial balance based on the normal balance of each account.

ABC Company
Trial Balance
January 31, 20X0

	Dr.	Cr.
Cash	$32,000	
Accounts Receivable		$ 5,000
Accounts Payable	3,000	
Share Capital		14,000
Sales	28,000	
Supplies Expense	1,000	
Salaries Expense	3,000	
Sales Expense		4,000
Total	$67,000	$23,000

ABC Company
Trial Balance
January 31, 20X0

	Dr.	Cr.
Cash	$	$
Accounts Receivable		
Accounts Payable		
Share Capital		
Sales		
Supplies Expense		
Salaries Expense		
Sales Expense		
Total	$	$

4-3

Financial information of ABC Company for December is presented below.

Dec. 1 Began business with $13,000 in cash and $5,000 in equipment and issued ordinary shares.

3 Bought additional equipment for $3,000 on account.

7 Purchased supplies for $1,600 cash.

12 Paid $1,500 to the creditor for the balance.

16 Received $3,400 in fees earned during the month.

23 Paid salary of part-time assistant, $400.

28 Paid balance due on equipment.

Enter the above transactions in the respective T-accounts below.

4-4

Using the above information, prepare a trial balance.

ABC Company
Trial Balance
December 31, 20X0

	Dr.	Cr.
	$	$
Total	$	$

4-5

Enter the following transactions into their respective T- accounts.

May 1   Mr. M. Owen opened his business, investing $5,000 in cash.

4   Bought supplies for cash, $400.

5   Bought furniture from ABC Company on account, $3,000.

15   Received $3,500 in fees earned during the month.

30   Paid salary for part-time help, $300.

30   Paid office rent for May, $1,500.

31   Paid $2,200 to ABC Company.

4-6

Using the above information, prepare a trial balance.

M. Owen
Trial Balance
May 31, 20X0

	Dr.	Cr.
	$	$
Total	$	$

4-7

Which of the following is the error that is not revealed by a trial balance?

(1) The accounts payable balance of €400 was not booked on the trial balance.
(2) A transaction involving the purchase of goods for €700 was not booked.
(3) Accrued expense of €1,000 was booked in the trial balance as a debit.
(4) The sales revenue of €800 was not booked.
(5) None of the above

4-8

The following is the trial balance for Mark Cleaning on July 31, 20X0:

Mark Cleaning
Trial Balance
July 31, 20X0

Cash	$10,000	
Accounts Receivable	20,000	
Furniture	700	
Equipment	1,500	
Accounts Payable		$ 8,800
Notes Payable		10,400
Share Capital		10,000
Retained Earnings		3,000
	$32,200	$32,200

Transactions for August were as follows:

Aug. 3 Paid $1,800 for accounts payable.

9 Paid $1,000 for notes payable.

13 Received $8,000 for cleaning income.

22 Bought equipment at a cost of $20,000 with a cash down payment of $7,000.

25 Paid professional fees of $2,000.

31 Invested additional cash of $5,000.

Using this information, prepare a trial balance for August 31, 20X0.

4-9

Prepare a trial balance as of December 31, 20X0 for D Company, using the following.

Cash	$ 9,400
Accounts receivable	1,000
Supplies	700
Equipment	900
Building	11,000
Accounts payable	10,000
Share capital	5,000
Retained earnings	1,000
Income from delivery	12,000
Insurance expense	3,000
Professional fees	2,000

Chapter 4

4-10

Post the following journal entries for E Company to the T-accounts below.

(a) Cash	8,000	
Share capital		8,000
(b) Office supplies	3,000	
Accounts payable		2,000
Cash		1,000
(c) Accounts receivable	500	
Cleaning income		500
(d) Rent expense	800	
Cash		800
(e) Accounts payable	1,000	
Cash		1,000

4-11

Using the above account balances, prepare a trial balance.

4-12

Rearrange the following steps in proper order.

I. Preparation of a trial balance

II. Posting to a general ledger

III. Occurrence of a transaction

IV. Journalizing an entry

(1) III — II — I —IV

(2) III — I —IV — II

(3) III —IV — I — II

(4) III — II —IV — I

(5) III —IV — II — I

4-13

The following information is available regarding the accounts of ABC Company on June 30, 20X0.

Cash	?
Accounts receivable	2,100
Land	10,000
Accounts payable	2,500
Share capital	20,000
Retained earnings	8,000
Sales	19,000
Purchases	16,000
Salaries expense	10,000

Compute the amount of cash and prepare ABC's trial balance. When an entry is made in either the debit or credit column, the other should remain blank except for "Total".

Account Title	Dr.	Cr. ($)
Cash		
Accounts receivable		
Land		
Accounts payable		
Share capital		
Retained earnings		
Sales		
Purchases		
Salaries expense		
Total		

4-14

In the above case, assume that the following transactions were not recorded:

Date	Transactions
5	Purchased $5,500 merchandise on account.
7	Received $1,000 cash in settlement of accounts receivable.
11	Sold merchandise for $8,000 cash.
20	Paid $2,000 cash for salaries.

Prepare the correct trial balance.

Account Title	Dr.	Cr. ($)
Cash		
Accounts receivable		
Land		
Accounts payable		
Share capital		
Retained earnings		
Sales		
Purchases		
Salaries expense		
Total		

4-15

On June 30, 20X2, the monthly trial balance of Kittel Company did not balance.

Kittel Company
Trial balance
June 30, 20X2

(€)

	Dr.	Cr.
Cash	5,200	
Accounts receivable	3,600	
Accounts payable		5,300
Share capital		2,000
Retained earnings		500
Sales		19,000
Salaries expense	13,100	
Rent expense	5,000	
	26,900	26,800

In reviewing the ledger and journals, the following errors were revealed.
- A cash payment of €1,000 for utilities expense was recorded as a debit to rent expense account.
- A cash receipt of €600 in settlement of an accounts receivable was debited to cash account for €800 and credited to accounts payable account for €800.
- A journal entry for a payment of €200 for salaries expense was debited to salaries expense account for €300.

Prepare a corrected trial balance.

Kittel Company
Trial balance
June 30, 20X2

(€)

	Dr.	Cr.
Cash		
Accounts receivable		
Accounts payable		
Share capital		
Retained earnings		
Sales		
Salaries expense		
Rent expense		
Utilities expense		

CHAPTER 5 ─決算修正仕訳─

難易度レベル ★ ★ ★

Adjusting Entries

Bookkeeping & Accounting Test for International Communication

BATIC

5-1

Post the following journal entries to the T-accounts below.

General Journal   G4

Date	Accounts	Dr.	Cr.
Feb. 11	Cash	170	
	Accounts Receivable		170
14	Accounts Receivable	500	
	Sales		500
17	Rent	300	
	Rent Payable		300
28	Rent Payable	150	
	Cash		150
29	Depreciation Expense	20	
	Accumulated Depreciation		20

5-2

Service fees were received in advance. These are for services to be rendered over the next 3 years. When should the fees received be reported as revenue?

(1) In the period when the fees are received.

(2) In the period when the services are performed.

(3) At the date the service starts.

(4) At the date the service ends.

(5) None of the above

5-3

On November 1, 20X0, Key Company paid $3,600 in premium for a three-year insurance policy. What amount should be reported for insurance expense in Key's financial statements for the year ended December 31, 20X0?

(1) $3,600

(2) $ 200

(3) $0

(4) $1,200

(5) None of the above

5-4

China Company assigns some of its patents to other companies under various agreements. Some royalties are received when the agreements are signed, the rest are remitted when each term ends. The following data are included in China's balance sheet as of December 31:

	20X1	20X2
Royalties receivable	$80,000	$90,000
Unearned royalties	45,000	50,000

During 20X2, China received royalty remittances of $250,000. In its income statement for the year ended December 31, 20X2, China should report royalty income of

(1) $200,000.

(2) $210,000.

(3) $235,000.

(4) $255,000.

(5) None of the above

5-5

Blue Company acquired a new plant asset on July 1, 20X0 at a cost of €700,000. It has an estimated 20-year service life and estimated residual value of €60,000. Blue's accounting period is the calendar year. Blue uses the straight-line depreciation method. In its 20X0 income statement, what amount should Blue report as depreciation expense for this plant asset?

(1) €0
(2) €16,000
(3) €32,000
(4) €35,000
(5) None of the above

5-6

Angela Company acquired equipment at a cost of $10,000 on July 1, 20X1. It is estimated that the equipment will have a useful life of 5 years and a residual value of $1,200. Angela uses the double-declining balance method. In its balance sheet as of December 31, 20X2, what amount should Angela report as accumulated depreciation for the equipment?

(1) $2,640
(2) $4,576
(3) $5,200
(4) $5,280
(5) None of the above

5-7

A 4-year rent agreement was made and $2,400 were paid on October 1, 20X0. The amount was debited to Prepaid Rent. Make the adjusting entry for the period ending December 31, 20X0.

5-8

ABC Company acquired an asset on January 1, 20X0 at a cost of $45,000, with an estimated useful life of 10 years and residual value of $3,000.

What is the annual depreciation expense based on the sum-of-the-years'-digits method for the year ended December 31, 20X0?

(1) $4,250
(2) $4,500
(3) $8,181
(4) $9,000
(5) None of the above

5-9

Office supplies costing $1,500 were debited to Office Supplies (an asset account). A count of the supplies at the end of the period showed $600 worth still on hand.

(a) Show the adjusting entry.
(b) Show the adjusting entry if the supplies were debited to a supplies expense account when purchased.

5-10

Weekly wages of $1,000 (5-day week) are paid to employees on Friday. The amount of the adjusting entry at the end of the fiscal period ending on Tuesday is

(1) $1,000
(2) $ 600
(3) $ 400
(4) $0
(5) None of the above

5-11

A supplies account on December 31 has a balance of $1,200 before adjustment. The year-end inventory showed $400 of supplies on hand. The amount of the adjusting entry is

(1) $ 400.
(2) $ 800.
(3) $1,200.
(4) $1,600.
(5) None of the above

5-12

Which of the following is correct as the adjusting entry to record depreciation of equipment?

(1) Dr. Depreciation expense   Cr. Accounts payable
(2) Dr. Depreciation expense   Cr. Accumulated depreciation
(3) Dr. Accumulated depreciation   Cr. Equipment
(4) Dr. Accounts payable   Cr. Depreciation expense
(5) None of the above

5-13

Which of the following is correct as an adjusting entry to record salaries owed to employees but not paid yet at the end of the year?

(1) Dr. Salaries payable   Cr. Salaries expense

(2) Dr. Cash   Cr. Salaries expense

(3) Dr. Salaries expense   Cr. Salaries payable

(4) No adjusting entry is needed.

(5) None of the above

5-14

A balance of prepaid insurance was $1,600 at the beginning of the fiscal year ending December 31, 20X1. A $3,200 annual premium had been paid on July 1, 20X0. A $2,000 annual insurance premium was paid on July 1, 20X1. In its December 31, 20X1 balance sheet, what amount should be reported as prepaid insurance?

(1) $1,000

(2) $2,000

(3) $2,600

(4) $3,600

(5) None of the above

5-15

ABC Company, a calendar-year company, bought office supplies for €3,000 on account and debited to an asset account. €400 of them remained unused at the end of the year.

When ABC Company bought the office supplies, which of the following journal entries did it make?

(1) Office supplies   3,000
      Cash   3,000

(2) Office supplies   3,000
      Accounts payable   3,000

(3) Cash   3,000
      Accounts payable   3,000

(4) Cash   3,000
      Office supplies   3,000

(5) Accounts payable   3,000
      Office supplies   3,000

5-16

In the above case, ABC Company made the correct adjusting entry at the end of the year. What is the effect of this adjusting entry on the amount of assets, liabilities, and equity?

	Assets	Liabilities	Equity
(1)	Decrease	Decrease	No effect
(2)	Decrease	No effect	Decrease
(3)	No effect	No effect	No effect
(4)	Increase	Increase	Decrease
(5)	Increase	No effect	Increase

5-17

On March 1, ABC Company, a calendar-year company, started to rent an office to XYZ Company and received $9,000 cash as annual rent fee. What amount of rent income should ABC Company report for the first year?

5-18

ABC Company, a calendar-year company, borrowed $12,000 from a bank on September 1. It will pay 9% interest annually on August 31 and repay the principal in three years. What amount of interest expense should ABC Company report for the first year? Assume that 1 year = 360 days.

Chapter 5

5-19

ABC Company had the following fixed assets.

Title	Acquisition date	Acquisition cost	Useful life	Salvage (residual) value	Depreciation method
Building	January 1, 20X3	$80,000	20 years	$10,000	Straight-line
Machinery	June 1, 20X4	$50,000	5 years	$5,000	Straight-line
Delivery Equipment	January 1, 20X5	$15,000	10 years	$2,000	Double-declining balance

ABC's fiscal year ends on December 31.

Compute the following amounts that ABC Company should report in its 20X5 financial statements.

(a) Depreciation expense of building

(b) Net book value of building

(c) Accumulated depreciation of machinery

(d) Depreciation expense of delivery equipment

5-20

The following is a trial balance of Company A.

Account Title	Dr.	Cr. ($)
Cash	18,300	
Accounts receivable	5,200	
Building	20,000	
Accounts payable		3,500
Share capital		20,000
Retained earnings		9,000
Sales		25,000
Salaries expense	14,000	
	57,500	57,500

Additional information for adjusting entries is as follows:

· Depreciation expense for 20X0 was $2,000.

· Salaries owed to employees but not paid was $3,000.

Complete the adjusted trial balance.

($)

Account Title	Trial Balance Dr.	Trial Balance Cr.	Adjustment Dr.	Adjustment Cr.	Adjusted Trial Balance Dr.	Adjusted Trial Balance Cr.
Cash	18,300					
Accounts receivable	5,200					
Building	20,000					
( )						
Accounts payable		3,500				
( )						
Share capital		20,000				
Retained earnings		9,000				
Sales		25,000				
Salaries expense	14,000					
( )						
Total	57,500	57,500				

5-21

On November 1, ABC company, a calendar-year company, lent XYZ company $12,000. It will receive 6% interest annually on October 31 and principal repayment in three years. Which of the following entries should ABC company make at the end of the first year? Assume that 1 year = 360 days.

(1) Cash   120
      Interest income   120
(2) Cash   2,160
      Interest income   2,160
(3) Interest receivable   120
      Interest income   120
(4) Interest receivable   2,160
      Interest income   2,160
(5) No journal entry is necessary.

5-22

ABC Company had the following fixed assets.

	Acquisition date	Acquisition cost	Useful life	Salvage (residual) value	Depreciation method
Building	January 1, 20X3	€100,000	10 years	€10,000	Straight-line
Delivery Equipment	January 1, 20X4	€15,000	5 years	€1,500	Double-declining balance
Office Equipment	January 1, 20X4	€120,000	10 years	€10,000	Sum-of-the-years'-digits

ABC's fiscal year ends on December 31.

Compute the following amounts that ABC Company should report in its 20X5 financial statements.

(a) Depreciation expense of building

(b) Net book value of building

(c) Depreciation expense of delivery equipment

(d) Accumulated depreciation of delivery equipment

(e) Depreciation expense of office equipment

Chapter 5

5-23

On October 3, 20X0, ABC Company, a calendar-year company, purchased $1,500 of office supplies with cash and debited to an expense account. On December 31, 20X0, $900 of them remained unused.

When ABC Company uses the reversing entry, which of the following entries should ABC Company make at the beginning of 20X1?

(1) Office supplies	600	
Office supplies expense		600
(2) Office supplies expense	600	
Office supplies		600
(3) Office supplies	900	
Office supplies expense		900
(4) Office supplies expense	900	
Office supplies		900
(5) No journal entry is necessary.		

CHAPTER 6 ―棚卸資産と売上原価の会計処理―

Accounting for Inventory and Cost of Sales

Bookkeeping & Accounting Test for International Communication

BATIC

6-1

Determine the cost of sales from the following information.

Beginning inventory	$5,000
Purchases during the period	3,700
Ending inventory	2,500

(1) $2,500

(2) $3,700

(3) $5,000

(4) $6,200

(5) None of the above

6-2

Based on the following information, determine the cost of sales.

Beginning Inventory	€ 2,000
Purchases during the period	30,000
Purchase discounts during the period	4,000
Freight-in on purchases during the period	1,000
Ending Inventory	3,000

(1) €24,000

(2) €26,000

(3) €27,000

(4) €29,000

(5) €30,000

6-3

C Company bought merchandise for cash. Indicate the correct journal entry under a periodic inventory system.

(1) Debit Merchandise, Credit Cash

(2) Debit Cash, Credit Purchases

(3) Debit Purchases, Credit Cash

(4) Debit Cash, Credit Merchandise

(5) None of the above

6-4

ABC Company uses a periodic inventory system. On May 1, it bought merchandise with $3,000 cash, and on June 30, it sold the merchandise for $8,000 cash.

(a) Make the journal entry on May 1.

    Dr.

        Cr.

(b) Make the journal entry on June 30.

    Dr.

        Cr.

Chapter 6

6-5

ABC Company, using a perpetual inventory system, had the following transactions.

Date	Transactions
August 3	Bought €5,000 merchandise on account.
20	Sold the above merchandise for €11,000 cash.

(a) Which of the following journal entries should ABC Company make on August 3?

    (1) Inventory   5,000
           Accounts payable   5,000

    (2) Inventory   5,000
           Cash   5,000

    (3) Inventory   5,000
           Purchases   5,000

    (4) Purchases   5,000
           Accounts payable   5,000

    (5) Purchases   5,000
           Cash   5,000

(b) Which of the following journal entries should ABC Company make on August 20?

(1) Accounts receivable   11,000
    Sales   11,000

(2) Cash   11,000
    Sales   11,000

(3) Accounts receivable   11,000
    Inventory   5,000
      Sales   11,000
      Cost of sales   5,000

(4) Cash   11,000
    Inventory   5,000
      Sales   11,000
      Purchases   5,000

(5) Cash   11,000
    Cost of sales   5,000
      Sales   11,000
      Inventory   5,000

Chapter 6

6-6

The following is a trial balance of ABC Company.

Account Title	Dr.	Cr. ($)
Cash	9,000	
Accounts receivable	5,600	
Inventory	1,000	
Building	18,000	
Accounts payable		2,500
Share capital		15,000
Retained earnings		2,000
Sales		30,000
Purchases	15,000	
Interest expense	900	
	49,500	49,500

Additional information for adjusting entries is as follows:

① Depreciation expense for 20X0 was $2,000.

② Inventory balance on December 31, 20X0 was $1,200.

Complete the adjusted trial balance.

($)

Account Title	Trial Balance Dr.	Trial Balance Cr.	Adjustment Dr.	Adjustment Cr.	Adjusted Trial Balance Dr.	Adjusted Trial Balance Cr.
Cash	9,000					
Accounts receivable	5,600					
Inventory	1,000					
Building	18,000					
Accumulated depreciation						
Accounts payable		2,500				
Share capital		15,000				
Retained earnings		2,000				
Sales		30,000				
Purchases	15,000					
Interest expense	900					
Income summary						
Depreciation expense						
Total	49,500	49,500				

6-7

ABC Company uses a periodic inventory system. On May 1, it bought merchandise with €8,000 cash, and on June 30, it sold the merchandise for €15,000 cash.

(a) Which of the following journal entries should ABC Company make on May 1?

    (1) Cash   8,000
            Inventory   8,000

    (2) Cash   8,000
            Purchases   8,000

    (3) Inventory   8,000
            Cash   8,000

    (4) Inventory   8,000
            Purchases   8,000

    (5) Purchases   8,000
            Cash   8,000

(b) Which of the following journal entries should ABC Company make on June 30?

(1) Cash   15,000
     Sales   15,000

(2) Sales   15,000
     Cash   15,000

(3) Cash   15,000
   Inventory   8,000
     Sales   15,000
     Cost of sales   8,000

(4) Cash   8,000
   Cost of sales   8,000
     Sales   8,000
     Inventory   8,000

(5) Cash   15,000
   Cost of sales   8,000
     Sales   15,000
     Inventory   8,000

6-8

ABC Company, a calendar-year company, had the following transactions during 20X0.

	Purchased	Sold
March 3	$1,000 (500 units×@$2)	
April 21		$2,000 (400 units × @$5)
July 28	$2,000 (1,000 units×@$2)	
September 10		$3,000 (600 units × @$5)
October 8	$1,000 (500 units×@$2)	
November 12		$4,000 (800 units × @$5)
December 19		$ 500 (100 units × @$5)

Beginning inventory was $200 (100 units × @$2) .

ABC Company uses a perpetual inventory system.

(a) Determine the following amounts on September 10.
- Sales
- Cost of sales

(b) Determine the following amounts for 20X0 financial statements.
- Sales
- Cost of sales
- Inventory

6-9

The following is taken from a record of Texas Corporation's transactions for the month of March 20X0:

Date	Transaction	Unit	Unit Cost	Total Cost	Unit on hand
3/1/20X0	Balance	400	$2	$ 800	400
3/7/20X0	Purchase	400	4	1,600	800
3/17/20X0	Sale	600			200
3/22/20X0	Purchase	800	5	4,000	1,000
3/26/20X0	Sale	300			700

Calculate the ending inventory using the following.

(1) First-in, first-out method

(2) Weighted-average method

(3) Moving-average method

CHAPTER 7 —精算表と締切仕訳—

Worksheet and
Closing Entries

Bookkeeping & Accounting Test for International Communication

BATIC

7-1

An Interest Expense account had a balance of $15,000 on December 31 before any necessary adjustment. Interest amount owed, but not yet paid is $500. Journalize the entries relating to the following.

(a) Accrued interest as of December 31.
(b) The closing of the interest expense account.

7-2

A trial balance shows the following balances at the end of the period. Journalize the closing entries for (a) income and (b) expenses.

Interest income	$12,000
Service income	5,000
Salaries expense	5,000
Interest expense	500
Depreciation expense	200
Rent expense	4,000

(a)

(b)

7-3

Journalize the adjustment entries that have been posted to the accounts presented in T-account forms below.

Cash	
5,000	

Supplies	
300	150

Prepaid Rent	
2,000	1,000

Building	
50,000	

Accumulated Depreciation	
	5,000

Interest Payable	
	500

Share Capital	
	40,000

Retained Earnings	
	6,300

Service Income	
	11,000

Interest Expense	
500	

Rent Expense	
1,000	

Depreciation Expense	
5,000	

Supplies Expense	
150	

7-4

Based on the above information, journalize the closing entries.

7-5

Based on the above information(7-3, 7-4), prepare a post-closing trial balance.

7-6

The following information is available regarding the accounts of ABC Company on December 31, 20X0.

Cash	$14,700
Notes receivable	3,000
Building	20,000
Bonds payable	10,000
Share capital	7,000
Retained earnings	4,000
Sales	30,000
Rent expense	1,300
Salaries expense	12,000

Determine the amount of profit for the year ended December 31, 20X0.

7-7

In the above case, complete the following post-closing trial balance. When an entry is made in either the debit or credit column, the other should remain blank except for "Total".

	Dr.	($) Cr.
Cash		
Notes receivable		
Building		
Bonds payable		
Share capital		
Retained earnings		
Total		

7-8

Make closing entries for the following accounts.

(a) Sales   €50,000

(b) Interest expense   3,000

(c) Cash   4,000

7-9

Rearrange the following steps in proper order.

1. Posting to a ledger
2. Preparation of a trial balance
3. Journalizing an entry
4. Occurrence of a transaction

7-10

From the following trial balance and adjustments information, prepare a worksheet.

T. Drew Company
Trial Balance
December 31, 20X0

Cash	$ 3,500	
Accounts Receivable	2,910	
Supplies	1,900	
Prepaid Rent	6,250	
Equipment	9,000	
Accounts Payable		$ 5,000
Notes Payable		6,000
Share Capital		6,000
Retained Earnings		2,000
Service Income		7,500
Salaries Expense	2,000	
Interest Expense	600	
General Expense	340	
	$26,500	$26,500

Adjustments:

(a) Depreciation for the year was $900.

(b) Supplies on hand at the end of the year were $800.

(c) Rent for the year was $500.

(d) Salaries owed but not paid yet were $900.

(e) Service rendered but not received fees was $300.

T. Drew Company
Worksheet
December 31, 20X0

Account Title	Trial Balance		Adjustments		Income Statement		Balance Sheet	
	Dr.	Cr.	Dr.	Cr.	Dr.	Cr.	Dr.	Cr.
Cash								
Accounts Receivable								
Supplies								
Prepaid Rent								
Equipment								
Accounts Payable								
Notes Payable								
Share Capital								
Retained Earnings								
Service Income								
Salaries Expense								
Interest Expense								
General Expense								
Depreciation Expense								
Accumulated Depreciation								
Supplies Expense								
Rent Expense								
Salaries Payable								
Profit								

7-11

From the above information, prepare all adjusting and closing entries.

Adjusting Entries

Closing Entries

7-12

From the above information(7-10, 7-11), prepare the income statement and balance sheet.

T. Drew Company
Income Statement
For the Period Ended December 31, 20X0

Service Income
Expenses:
  Salaries Expense
  Interest Expense
  General Expense
  Depreciation Expense
  Supplies Expense
  Rent Expense   _____
Total Expenses   _____
Profit

T. Drew Company
Balance Sheet
As of December 31, 20X0

ASSETS		LIABILITIES AND EQUITY	
Current Assets:		Liabilities:	
Cash		Accounts Payable	
Accounts Receivable		Notes Payable	
Supplies		Salaries Payable	_____
Prepaid Rent	_____	Total Liabilities	
Total Current Assets		Equity:	
Non-current Assets:		Share Capital	
Equipment		Retained Earnings	_____
Less: Accumulated Dep.	_____ _____	Total Equity	_____
		Total Liabilities	
Total Assets	_____	and Equity	_____

7-13

Based on the following trial balance of Rose Company and information for the adjustments, prepare a worksheet.

Rose Company
Trial Balance
December 31, 20X0

Cash	$16,000	
Accounts Receivable	18,000	
Merchandise Inventory	4,400	
Supplies	660	
Prepaid Insurance	900	
Equipment	17,000	
Accumulated Depreciation		$ 3,000
Accounts Payable		7,860
Notes Payable		8,800
Share Capital		10,000
Retained Earnings		7,000
Sales		47,700
Purchases	18,300	
Advertising Expense	4,200	
Rent Expense	3,600	
Miscellaneous Expense	1,300	
	$84,360	$84,360

Adjustments:

(a) Merchandise inventory on December 31, 20X0 was $2,700.

(b) Supplies on hand at the end of the year were $400.

(c) Depreciation expense for the year 20X0 was $1,000.

(d) Insurance expense for this year was $400.

Rose Company
Worksheet
December 31, 20X0

Account Title	Trial Balance		Adjustments		Income Statement		Balance Sheet	
	Dr.	Cr.	Dr.	Cr.	Dr.	Cr.	Dr.	Cr.
Cash								
Accounts Receivable								
Merchandise Inventory								
Supplies								
Prepaid Insurance								
Equipment								
Accumulated Depreciation								
Accounts Payable								
Notes Payable								
Share Capital								
Retained Earnings								
Sales								
Purchases								
Advertising Expense								
Rent Expense								
Miscellaneous Expense								
Income Summary								
Depreciation Expense								
Supplies Expense								
Insurance Expense								
Profit								

7-14

Regarding the accounting cycle, which of the following descriptions is correct?

(1) After financial statements are prepared, an income summary is set up to make adjusting entries.

(2) A trial balance is the schedule for the initial entry of accounting information.

(3) In order to prove the mathematical equality of debt and credit after posting, adjusting entries are made.

(4) The balances of revenue accounts and expense accounts are reduced to zero through the recording of closing entries.

(5) The step of transferring information from a ledger to a journal is called posting.

CHAPTER 8 ―財務諸表―

Financial Statements

Bookkeeping & Accounting Test for International Communication

BATIC

8-1

The information relating to ABC Company was as follows at the end of the accounting period.

Sales	$220,000
Purchases returns and allowances	300
Inventory (beginning)	50,000
Inventory (ending)	45,000
Freight on purchases	3,000
Purchases	198,000

Calculate:

(a) Net purchases

(b) Cost of sales

(c) Gross profit

8-2

Prepare an income statement by using the information below.

Fees income	$4,000
Advertising expense	600
Salaries expense	1,200
Rent expense	780

8-3

Based on the following information, prepare an income statement.

Service income	€15,000
Insurance expense	3,000
Rent expense	1,500
Salaries expense	1,000

8-4

Which of the following accounts is classified into current assets?

(1) Equipment

(2) Inventory

(3) Land

(4) Notes payable

(5) None of the above

8-5

Which of the following accounts is classified into non-current assets?

(1) Cash

(2) Accounts payable

(3) Share capital

(4) Land

(5) None of the above

8-6

Which of the following accounts is classified into current liabilities?

(1) Prepaid rent
(2) Salaries payable
(3) Accounts receivable
(4) Salaries expense
(5) None of the above

8-7

Which of the following accounts is classified into non-current liabilities?

(1) Bonds payable
(2) Accounts payable
(3) Accounts receivable
(4) Land
(5) None of the above

8-8

Prepare a classified balance sheet as of December 31, 20X0 for SSS Company based upon the following assets, liabilities, and equity.

Cash	€6,700
Accounts payable	7,000
Vehicles	1,600
Accounts receivable	800
Equipment	5,800
Equity	7,900

8-9

Compute the amounts of net sales, gross profit, and operating profit based on the following information.

Sales	$30,000
Sales returns and allowances	1,300
Sales discounts	200
Cost of sales	8,000
Operating expense	5,000

8-10

Compute the cost of sales based on the following information.

Purchases	$10,000
Purchase returns and allowances	800
Purchase discounts	100
Freight on purchases	1,200
Beginning inventory	1,500
Ending inventory	1,800

8-11

The following information is available regarding the accounts of ABC Company on December 31, 20X0.

Accounts Title	Amount
Cash	$ 7,000
Accounts receivable	5,500
Inventory	4,000
Land	20,000
Loans payable	4,000
Share capital	4,500
Retained earnings	3,000
Sales	68,000
Purchases	35,000
Salaries expense	8,000

Additional information for adjusting entries is as follows:
- Inventory balance on December 31, 20X0 was $4,300.
- ABC borrowed $4,000 from a bank on October 1, 20X0. Interest expense of $70 should be accrued for the year ended December 31, 20X0.

Prepare ABC's income statement for the year ended December 31, 20X0. Select appropriate account titles and/or descriptions from the list below.

1. Purchases	2. Land	3. Cost of sales
4. Profit	5. Interest expense	6. Gross profit
7. Retained earnings	8. Interest payable	9. Inventory

ABC Company
Income Statement
For the Year Ended December 31, 20X0

Sales		$ [ ]
[ ]		[ ]
[ ]		[ ]
Salaries expense		[ ]
[ ]		[ ]
[ ]		$ [ ]

8-12

In the above case, prepare ABC's balance sheet as of December 31, 20X0. Select appropriate account titles and/or descriptions from the list below.

1. Purchases	2. Land	3. Cost of sales
4. Profit	5. Interest expense	6. Gross profit
7. Retained earnings	8. Interest payable	9. Inventory

ABC Company
Balance Sheet
As of December 31, 20X0

Assets		Liabilities and Equity	
Cash	$ 7,000	Loans payable	$ [ ]
Accounts receivable	5,500	[ ]	[ ]
[ ]	[ ]	Total liabilities	[ ]
[ ]	[ ]	Share capital	4,500
		Retained earnings	[ ]
		Total equity	[ ]
		Total liabilities and	
Total assets	$ [ ]	equity	$ [ ]

8-13

Fill in appropriate account titles and/or descriptions.

ABC Company
Income Statement
For the Year Ended December 31, 20X0

Net sales	$ 45,990
Cost of sales	23,300
(1)	22,690
Selling, general and administrative expense	9,083
(2)	13,607
Interest expense	5,990
profit before income tax	7,617
Income tax	3,045
(3)	$ 4,572

8-14

Select appropriate account titles and/or descriptions from the list below.

ABC Company
Balance Sheet
As of December 31, 20X0

Assets			Liabilities and Equity	
Current assets:			Current liabilities:	
Cash	$2,360		(3)	$4,290
Short-term investments	2,400		Salaries payable	703
Accounts receivable	500		Income tax payable	520
(1)	460		Total current liabilities	5,513
Prepaid interest	520			
Total current assets	6,240		Non-current liabilities:	
			(4)	640
Non-current assets:				
(2)	15,000		Total liabilities	6,153
Less accumulated depreciation	(3,120)			
Total non-current assets	11,880		Equity:	
			Share capital	4,000
			(5)	7,967
			Total equity	11,967
Total assets	$18,120		Total liabilities and equity	$18,120

Equipment, Retained earnings, Bonds payable, Inventory, Accounts payable

8-15

ABC Company recorded profit of $17,000 for the year ended December 31, 20X0. The tax rate is 25%. What amount of income tax expense should ABC Company recognize for the year ended December 31, 20X0?

8-16

XYZ Company recorded profit of $35,000 for the year ended December 31, 20X0. The tax rate is 30%. Complete the following journal entry to recognize income tax expense for the year ended December 31, 20X0.

Income tax expense   [   ]

                                                    [   ]

8-17

ABC Company had retained earnings of $10,000 as of December 31, 20X4 and profit of $3,300 during 20X5. What amount of retained earnings should it report in its balance sheet as of December 31, 20X5?

8-18

In the above case, ABC Company had loss of $1,700 during 20X6. What amount of retained earnings should it report in its balance sheet as of December 31, 20X6?

8-19

ABC Company declared cash dividends of $5,000. Which of the following journal entries should it make?

(1) Dividends expense   5,000
        Cash   5,000
(2) Dividends expense   5,000
        Dividends payable   5,000
(3) Retained earnings   5,000
        Cash   5,000
(4) Retained earnings   5,000
        Dividends payable   5,000
(5) No journal entry is necessary.

8-20

On December 31, 20X5, ABC Company declared cash dividends of €10,000, and on January 20, 20X6, it paid the dividends. Make the journal entry on January 20, 20X6.

CHAPTER 9 ―基本的な前提とGAAP―

Basic Assumptions and GAAP

Bookkeeping & Accounting Test for International Communication

BATIC

9-1

Standards, conventions, and rules that accountants follow in recording transactions and in the preparation of financial statements are called (   ).

9-2

Which of the following assumptions, principles, or constraints most appropriately justifies the practice that expenses are recognized not when wages are paid but when the service actually makes its contribution to revenue?

(1) Matching principle

(2) Revenue recognition principle

(3) Conservatism

(4) Historical cost principle

(5) None of the above

9-3

Which of the following is the assumption that a company will continue in operation for the foreseeable future?

(1) Economic entity assumption

(2) Periodicity assumption

(3) Going concern assumption

(4) Monetary unit assumption

(5) None of the above

9-4

What does GAAP stand for?

(1) Generally Accepted Accounting Principles

(2) Generally Anticipated Accounting Principles

(3) Globally Accepted Accounting Principles

(4) Globally Anticipated Accounting Principles

(5) None of the above

9-5

International Financial Reporting Standards are set by

(1) FASB.

(2) IAS.

(3) IASB.

(4) IOSCO.

(5) SEC.

CHAPTER 10 ―財務諸表分析―

Financial Statement Analysis

Bookkeeping & Accounting Test for International Communication

BATIC

10-1

Which is the more profitable company?

	Company A	Company B
Profit margin	5%	8%

10-2

Based on the following information, calculate the inventory turnover.

Cost of sales	$46,000
Inventory	2,000

10-3

Based on the following information, calculate the quick ratio.

Current assets	$6,000
Inventory	1,000
Current liabilities	4,000

10-4

Which company is more able to meet short-term obligation?

	Company A	Company B
Current assets	$45,000	$70,000
Current liabilities	$40,000	$50,000

10-5

Did the company's financial structure improve or deteriorate for creditors?

	20X0	20X1
Liabilities	$5,500	$7,000
Equity	$6,000	$8,000

10-6

From the shareholders' viewpoint, which company is better?

	Company A	Company B
Profit	$1,000	$ 4,000
Equity	$5,000	$50,000

10-7

Which of the following shows ROA?

(1) Assets ÷ Return

(2) Assets − Return

(3) Assets × Return

(4) Return ÷ Assets

(5) Return − Assets

10-8

The following data are extracted from financial statements of Kante Company.

Sales	€40,000
Cost of sales	22,000
Profit	3,000
Total assets	32,000
Total liabilities	7,000
Equity	25,000

Based on the above data, calculate the following ratios.

(a) Profit margin
(b) ROE
(c) Total assets turnover ratio

CHAPTER 11 ―内部統制―

Internal Control

Bookkeeping & Accounting Test for International Communication

BATIC

11-1

Which of the following objectives do internal controls help to achieve?

(1) Reliability of financial reporting
(2) Effectiveness of operations
(3) Compliance with laws
(4) Efficiency of operations
(5) All of the above

11-2

Regarding the internal control system, choose the inapproriate description from the following.

(1) It is preferable to restrict access of cash to as few people as possible.
(2) Segregation of functions of record keeping and custody of assets is preferable.
(3) Definition of job responsibilities is required.
(4) To prevent the fraud, functions of placing orders, receiving merchandise, and paying vendors are to be segregated.
(5) In order to achieve the budget, the growth of sales amount is required.

11-3

On Jan 1, ABC Company established an imprest petty cash system of $100.
Journalize this transaction.

    Dr.
        Cr.

11-4

In January, ABC Company paid office supplies of $12, transportation of $28, freight of $32, charity of $8, and miscellaneous expense of $8 from a petty cash box. The petty cash box contained $12 at the end of the month. Journalize these transactions.

    Dr.
        Cr.

11-5

An imprest petty cash system is established for:

(1) Asset purchases
(2) Cash receipts
(3) Interest receipts and payments
(4) Sales transactions
(5) Small payments

11-6

In preparing the bank reconciliation as of June 30, 20X0 for Dien Company, the following information is available:

Balance per bank statement, 6/30/20X0	$3,500
Balance per book, 6/30/20X0	2,730
Outstanding checks, 6/30/20X0	800
Deposit in transit, 6/30/20X0	300
Unrecorded bank service charges for June	15
Unrecorded note collected by bank	240

Dien also found that its bookkeeper recorded its disbursement of June 12 as $294 instead of $249.

At June 30, 20X0, Dien's correct cash balance is

(1) $2,230
(2) $2,455
(3) $3,000
(4) $3,225
(5) None of the above

CHAPTER 12 —資産と負債の会計処理—

Accounting for Assets and Liabilities

Bookkeeping & Accounting Test for International Communication

BATIC

12-1

Due to the needs of its business operation, Jackson Company purchased a machine for $72,000 on January 1, 20X4. In addition to the purchase price, the following expenditures were incurred relating to the machine during 20X4.

Freight on purchase	$3,600
Costs of bringing and installing the machine to the place of intended operation	2,900
Costs of testing whether the machine is functioning properly while bringing it to the condition to be capable of intended operation	4,400
Costs of testing after the machine is functioning properly after bringing it to the condition to be capable of intended operation	2,700
Maintenance costs of day-to-day servicing of the machine	1,500

On Jackson's accounting book, what amount should be recorded as the cost of the machine?

(1) $75,600
(2) $82,900
(3) $84,400
(4) $85,600
(5) $87,100

12-2

ABC Company sold its old equipment to XYZ Company for $100,000 on November 1, 20X0. The equipment was originally acquired at a cost of $150,000, with residual value of $15,000. The accumulated depreciation as of November 1, 20X0 was $54,000. What amount should ABC recognize as gain (loss) on the sale?

(1) $(19,000)
(2) $ 0
(3) $ 4,000
(4) $ 11,000
(5) $ 100,000

12-3

BBB Ltd issued the following straight bonds.

Issue date	January 1, 20X1
Mature date	December 31, 20X4
Face amount	$80,000
Face rate	4%
Yield rate	5%
Payment of interest	Annually on December 31

Calculate the following amounts. Round each amount to the nearest dollar, if necessary.

(1) Issue price
(2) Interest expense for the year ended December 31, 20X1
(3) Discount on bonds payable as of December 31, 20X1

総合練習問題

Bookkeeping & Accounting Test for International Communication

BATIC

1

Select the most appropriate number to fill in the following blank.

A person who owes money is called [＿＿＿＿＿＿].

① Creditor
② Debtor
③ Depositor
④ Employer
⑤ Shareholder

2

ABC Company has equity of $80,000 and assets of $ 93,000. What is the amount of ABC's liabilities?

① $0
② $ 13,000
③ $ 40,000
④ $ 86,000
⑤ $173,000

3

Mr. Black founded XYZ Company by investing $25,000 cash and at the same time XYZ issued the equivalent ordinary shares. Subsequently, XYZ bought equipment for $15,000 cash. What is the amount of XYZ's assets?

① $10,000
② $15,000
③ $25,000
④ $30,000
⑤ $40,000

4

ABC Company acquired equipment at a cost of €80,000 and paid €10,000 cash on September 1. It paid the balance on September 30. Which of the following journal entries should ABC Company make on September 1?

① Equipment	80,000	
Cash		10,000
Accounts payable		70,000
② Cash	10,000	
Accounts payable	70,000	
Equipment		80,000
③ Equipment	80,000	
Accounts payable		80,000
④ Accounts payable	70,000	
Cash		70,000
⑤ Cash	70,000	
Accounts payable		70,000

ABC Company borrowed $50,000 from a bank. Which of the following journal entries should it make?

① Cash   50,000
        Loans   50,000
② Loans   50,000
        Cash   50,000
③ Cash   50,000
        Accounts payable   50,000
④ Accounts payable   50,000
        Cash   50,000
⑤ Loans   50,000
        Accounts payable   50,000

Salaries Expense		Cash	
1,000			1,000

Which of the following appropriately describes the above transaction?

① Bought merchandise.
② Paid an expense.
③ Purchased supplies.
④ Received cash.
⑤ Sold merchandise.

Questions 7 and 8 are based on the following:

ABC Company sold €700 of merchandise to XYZ Company for cash.

7

Which of the following journal entries should ABC Company make?

① Sales   700
    Cash   700
② Sales   700
    Accounts receivable   700
③ Cash   700
    Sales   700
④ Accounts receivable   700
    Sales   700
⑤ Cash   700
    Accounts receivable   700

8

Which of the following journal entries should XYZ Company should make?

① Accounts payable 700
   Purchases 700
② Accounts payable 700
   Cash 700
③ Cash 700
   Purchases 700
④ Purchases 700
   Accounts payable 700
⑤ Purchases 700
   Cash 700

XYZ Company issued an interest-bearing note of $10,000, 45 days from the date, at face value. The annual interest rate was 12%. When it settles the note, which of the following journal entries should it make? Assume that 1 year = 360 days.

① Cash   10,150
    Notes payable   10,000
    Interest expense   150
② Cash   11,200
    Notes payable   10,000
    Interest expense   1,200
③ Notes payable   10,000
    Cash   10,000
④ Notes payable   10,000
  Interest expense   150
    Cash   10,150
⑤ Notes payable   10,000
  Interest expense   1,200
    Cash   11,200

10

ABC Company sold merchandise to XYZ Company for $6,000 with the discount terms of 5%, 30 days on November 1. If XYZ pays on November 20, how much should it pay to ABC?

① $5,700
② $5,800
③ $5,975
④ $5,983
⑤ $6,000

Questions 11 and 12 are based on the following:

XYZ Company sold merchandise for €20,000 cash on August 1. Since the customer complained that part of the merchandise was damaged, XYZ refunded €900 cash on September 20.

11

Which of the following journal entries should XYZ Company make on August 1?

① Accounts receivable   19,100
     Sales   19,100
② Accounts receivable   20,000
     Sales   20,000
③ Cash   19,100
     Sales   19,100
④ Cash   20,000
     Sales   20,000
⑤ Cash   19,100
     Sales returns and allowances   900
         Sales   20,000

12

Which of the following journal entries should XYZ Company make on September 20?

① Cash   19,100

     Sales   19,100

② Sales   900

     Sales returns and allowances   900

③ Sales returns and allowances   900

     Cash   900

④ Sales returns and allowances   900

     Sales   900

⑤ No journal entry is necessary.

13

ABC Company sold merchandise for $2,000 on account on November 5. It received a promissory note for the account receivable on November 21.

Which of the following journal entries should ABC Company make on November 21?

① Accounts receivable   2,000
     Notes receivable   2,000

② Accounts receivable   2,000
     Sales   2,000

③ Cash   2,000
     Accounts receivable   2,000

④ Notes receivable   2,000
     Accounts receivable   2,000

⑤ Sales   2,000
     Accounts receivable   2,000

14

Interest receivable		Interest income	
1,000			1,000

Which of the following appropriately describes the above transaction?

① Accrued revenue.

② Accrued expense.

③ Received interest.

④ Received cash.

⑤ Paid interest.

15

Retained earnings   52,000

    Dividends payable   52,000

Which of the following appropriately describes the above journal entry?

① Declared dividends.

② Refunded dividends.

③ Received dividends.

④ Returned dividends.

⑤ Paid dividends.

16

ABC Company had retained earnings of $6,000 as of December 31, 20X4 and loss of $800 during 20X5. What amount of retained earnings should it report in its balance sheet as of December 31, 20X5?

① $ 800
② $5,200
③ $6,000
④ $6,500
⑤ $6,800

17

ABC Company, a calendar-year company, bought a one-year fire insurance policy and paid $1,200 on May 1, 20X0. What amount of insurance expense should be reported for the year ended December 31, 20X0?

① $0
② $ 400
③ $ 600
④ $ 800
⑤ $1,200

XYZ Company, a calendar-year company, acquired equipment at a cost of $8,000 on September 1, 20X0. XYZ used the straight-line method for depreciation and estimated the equipment's useful life of 5 years and residual value of $2,000. What amount of depreciation expense should XYZ Company record for the year ended December 31, 20X0?

① $0
② $　400
③ $　533
④ $1,200
⑤ $1,600

| 19 |

ABC Company, a calendar-year company, borrowed €72,000 at 8% annual interest on December 1, 20X0. Interest is to be paid at the maturity date in a year. Which of the following journal entries should ABC Company make on December 31, 20X0? Assume that 1 year = 360 days.

① Cash	480	
Interest expense		480
② Interest expense	5,760	
Cash		5,760
③ Interest expense	480	
Interest payable		480
④ Interest expense	5,760	
Interest payable		5,760
⑤ No journal entry is necessary.		

Questions 20 and 21 are based on the following:

ABC Company uses a periodic inventory system. On May 1, it bought merchandise with $300 on account and, on June 30, sold the merchandise for $700 cash.

総合練習問題

20

Which of the following journal entries should ABC Company make on May 1?

① Inventory   300
    Accounts payable   300
② Inventory   300
    Cash   300
③ Inventory   300
    Purchases   300
④ Purchases   300
    Accounts payable   300
⑤ Purchases   300
    Cash   300

Which of the following journal entries should ABC Company make on June 30?

① Cash   700

     Sales   700

② Sales   700

     Cash   700

③ Cash   700

   Inventory   300

     Sales   700

     Cost of sales   300

④ Cash   700

   Cost of sales   700

     Sales   700

     Inventory   700

⑤ Cash   700

   Cost of sales   300

     Sales   700

     Inventory   300

22

Compute the cost of sales based on the following information.

Purchases	$65,000
Beginning inventory	4,000
Ending inventory	2,800
Freight on purchases	8,700
Purchase returns and allowances	1,500

① $65,000

② $71,000

③ $72,200

④ $73,400

⑤ $90,800

Questions 23 and 24 are based on the following:

ABC Company had the following account balances as of October 31 and transactions during November.

Account balances as of October 31

Cash $10,000
Accounts receivable   3,000

Transactions during November

  1 Paid $1,500 cash for office supplies.
  2 Received $2,000 cash for settlement of accounts receivable.
  2 Sold merchandise for $5,000 on account.
10 Paid $150 cash for utilities.
13 Received $3,000 cash for settlement of accounts receivable.
18 Sold merchandise for $4,000 cash.
25 Sold merchandise for $1,000 on account.

23

What amount should be the cash balance as of November 30?

① $ 8,350
② $ 8,500
③ $16,850
④ $17,000
⑤ $17,350

24

What amount should be the accounts receivable balance as of November 30?

① $1,000
② $2,000
③ $3,000
④ $4,000
⑤ $5,000

25

Into which of the following categories should accounts payable be classified?

① Current assets
② Current liabilities
③ Non-current assets
④ Non-current liabilities
⑤ Equity

26

Which of the following is classified into current assets?

① Land
② Accounts payable
③ Accounts receivable
④ Equipment
⑤ Share capital

27

Rearrange the following steps in proper order.

(1) Posting to a general ledger

(2) Preparation of a trial balance

(3) Journalizing an entry

(4) Occurrence of a transaction

① (3) — (4) — (1) — (2)

② (3) — (4) — (2) — (1)

③ (4) — (2) — (3) — (1)

④ (4) — (3) — (2) — (1)

⑤ (4) — (3) — (1) — (2)

28

Fill in the following blank.

Adjusting entries are necessary, because financial statements are recorded on [   ].

① An accrual basis

② An asset basis

③ A cash basis

④ An equity basis

⑤ A liability basis

29

A company, in principle, uses [   ] to pay small amounts for miscellaneous expenses for the purpose of internal control.

Select the most appropriate number to fill in the above blank.

① An accounting system

② An imprest petty cash system

③ A periodic inventory system

④ A perpetual inventory system

⑤ A single-entry bookkeeping system

30

Moscon Company had the following information regarding the bank reconciliation as of May 31.

Balance of check account per book	€4,500
Not-Sufficient-Funds check returned	220
Unrecorded notes collected by bank	390

Calculate Moscon's correct balance of check account as of May 31.

The following are ABC Company's transactions during January.

Date	Transactions
10	Purchased $10,000 merchandise with cash.
20	Received $3,000 cash and a note of $7,000 for settlement of accounts receivable.
30	Sold merchandise for $6,000 on account.

31

Make the journal entries by selecting appropriate numbers from the list below.

```
1/10  Dr. (          )  10,000
           Cr. (          )        10,000


1/20  Dr. (          )   3,000
          (          )   7,000
           Cr. (          )        10,000


1/30  Dr. (          )   6,000
           Cr. (          )         6,000
```

1. Accounts payable	2. Purchase returns and allowances
3. Purchases	4. Cash 5. Accounts receivable
6. Notes receivable	7. Sales 8. Sales returns and allowances

32

Enter the transactions in T-accounts below. For account titles, select appropriate numbers from the list below. Fill in the account titles and amounts only.

---

1. Accounts payable   2. Purchase returns and allowances

3. Purchases   4. Cash   5. Accounts receivable

6. Notes receivable   7. Sales   8. Sales returns and allowances

XYZ Company had the following transaction.

August 20	XYZ returned merchandise to the seller in the amount of $400. The merchandise was previously bought on account.

Make the journal entry and then post to the ledger. Fill in appropriate account name, P.R. (posting reference) and amount in each space. Leave "Explanation" and "Balance" columns of ledger accounts blank.

General Journal   J6

Date	Account and Explanation	P.R.	Dr.	Cr.
Aug. 20				

Accounts payable   201

Date	Explanation	P.R.	Debit	Credit	Balance
Aug. 20					

Purchase returns   511

Date	Explanation	P.R.	Debit	Credit	Balance
Aug. 20					

34

ABC Company had the following fixed assets.

	Acquisition date	Acquisition cost	Useful life	Salvage (residual) value	Depreciation method
Building	January 1, 20X2	$120,000	10 years	$10,000	Straight-line
Office Equipment	January 1, 20X4	$6,000	5 years	$600	Double-declining balance
Machinery	January 1, 20X5	$15,000	5 years	$1,500	Sum-of-the-years'-digits

ABC's fiscal year ends on December 31.

Compute the following amounts that ABC should report in its 20X5 financial statements.

1. Depreciation expense of building　　　　　$[　　　　　]
2. Accumulated depreciation of building　　　$[　　　　　]
3. Depreciation expense of office equipment　$[　　　　　]
4. Depreciation expense of machinery　　　　$[　　　　　]

The following information is available regarding the accounts of ABC Company on December 31, 20X0.

Account Title	Amount
Cash	€ 8,000
Accounts receivable	2,000
Building	7,000
Accounts payable	?
Bonds payable	2,000
Share capital	4,000
Retained earnings	2,000
Sales	30,000
Purchases	20,000
Expenses	2,000

Determine the amount of accounts payable and complete ABC's trial balance. When an entry is made in either the debit or credit column, the other should remain blank except for "Total".

ABC Company
Trial Balance
December 31, 20X0

(€)

Account Title	Dr.	Cr.
Cash	[8,000]	[ ]
Accounts receivable	[2,000]	[ ]
Building	[7,000]	[ ]
Accounts payable	[ ]	[1,000]
Bonds payable	[ ]	[2,000]
Share capital	[ ]	[4,000]
Retained earnings	[ ]	[2,000]
Sales	[ ]	[30,000]
Purchases	[20,000]	[ ]
Expenses	[2,000]	[ ]
Total	[39,000]	[39,000]

The following financial data are from financial statements of Company A and of Company B.

	Company A	Company B
Sales	$ 88,000	$54,000
Profit for the year	5,000	4,000
Current assets	4,000	4,000
Non-current assets	109,000	90,000
Current liabilities	3,000	4,000
Non-current liabilities	40,000	10,000
Equity	70,000	80,000

If necessary, round numbers to one decimal place.

(1) Calculate the numbers for [   ] and circle the right answer in (   ).

Because Company A's profit margin is [   ] % while Company B's profit margin is [   ] %, Company (A   B) is more profitable.

(2) Calculate the numbers for [   ] and circle the right answer in (   ).

Because Company A's ROE is [   ] % while Company B's ROE is [   ] %, Company (A   B) is better for shareholders.

(3) Which company is more able to meet short-term obligation? Circle the right answer.

Company A   Company B

Questions 37 and 38 are based on the following:

The following information is available regarding the accounts of ABC Company on December 31, 20X0.

Account Title	Amount
Cash	$ 7,000
Accounts receivable	4,000
Inventory	2,500
Office supplies	1,000
Land	11,000
Accounts payable	4,000
Share capital	5,000
Retained earnings	3,000
Sales	41,500
Purchases	18,000
Rent expense	10,000

Additional information for adjusting entries is as follows:

(1) Inventory balance on December 31, 20X0 was $1,200.

(2) Office supplies costing $1,000 were debited to an asset account when purchased. $400 of them remained unused on December 31, 20X0.

37

Prepare ABC Company's income statement for the year ended December 31, 20X0. Select appropriate account titles and/or descriptions from the list below.

1. Gross profit	2. Inventory	3. Cost of sales
4. Purchases	5. Office supplies expense	
6. Profit	7. Retained earnings	8. Land

ABC Company
Income Statement
For the Year Ended December 31, 20X0

Sales	$ 41,500
_____	[ ]
_____	[ ]
Rent expense	10,000
_____	[ ]
_____	$ [ ]

38

Prepare ABC Company's balance sheet as of December 31, 20X0. Select appropriate account titles and/or descriptions from the list below.

1. Gross Profit	2. Inventory	3. Cost of sales
4. Purchases	5. Office supplies expense	
6. Profit	7. Retained earnings	8. Land

ABC Company
Balance Sheet
As of December 31, 20X0

Assets			Liabilities and Equity		
Cash	$	7,000	Accounts payable	$	4,000
Accounts receivable		4,000	Total liabilities		4,000
_____	[	]	Share capital	[	]
Office supplies	[	]	_____	[	]
_____	[	]	Total equity	[	]
Total assets	$ [	]	Total liabilities and equity	$ [	]

Basic Concepts
of Bookkeeping

Bookkeeping & Accounting Test for International Communication

BATIC

1-1

和訳 次のうち、資本を減額するものはどれか。

(1) 家具を掛けで購入した。

(2) 役務を行って、報酬を得た。

(3) 事務用文房具を現金で購入し、資産として記録した。

(4) 事務用文房具を現金で購入し、費用として記録した。

(5) 銀行から $5,000 借り入れた。

解答 (4)

1-2

和訳 B. ウェールズ氏は自分の会社に現金で出資し、事業を始めた。この取引は会社にとって、

(1) 資産増加、負債増加

(2) 資産増加、資本増加

(3) 資産減少、資本増加

(4) 資産増加、負債減少

(5) 影響なし

解答 (2)

1-3

和訳 A 社は機械を掛けで買った。この取引は、

(1) 資産増加、別の資産減少

(2) 資産増加、資本増加

(3) 資産増加、負債増加

(4) 資産減少、負債減少

(5) 負債増加、資本減少

解答 (3)

解説 機械の購入は、資産の増加であり、その購入が掛けの場合、負債（支払債務）を増加させる。

1-4

和訳 B 社は、債務を返済した。この取引は、

(1) 資産増加、負債増加

(2) 資産減少、負債減少

(3) 資産減少、資本減少

(4) 資産増加、別の資産減少

(5) 資産減少、資本増加

解答 (2)

解説 Accounts Payable（買掛金）を現金で支払った場合の仕訳は以下のとおり。

Dr. Accounts Payable ← 負債の減少

Cr. Cash ← 資産の減少

1-5

和訳 B 社は現金で備品を購入した。

この取引が資産、負債、資本の額へ与える影響は次のうちどれか。

	資産	負債	資本
(1)	増加	増減なし	増加
(2)	増加	増加	増減なし
(3)	減少	減少	増減なし
(4)	減少	増減なし	減少
(5)	増減なし	増減なし	増減なし

解答 (5)

解説 Cash (Asset) が Equipment (Asset) に入れ替わっただけなので、No Effect（増減なし）。

1-6

和訳 バー社は火災保険の保険料 $100 を支払った。この取引の仕訳をしなさい。

解答

Insurance Expense	100	
Cash		100

1-7

和訳　鈴木氏は $5,000 の現金、$3,000 相当の消耗品、$10,000 の価値の設備と、その設備のための支払手形 $5,000 を出資して事業を始めた。資本はいくらか。

(1)　$ 5,000

(2)　$13,000

(3)　$18,000

(4)　$23,000

(5)　上記のいずれでもない

解答　(2)

解説　　　　　　　資産　　　　　　＝負債　　＋資本

$5,000 + $3,000 + $10,000 = $5,000 + $13,000

1-8

和訳　当期中に資産総額が€3,000 増加し、資本も€1,000 増加した場合、負債総額に与える影響はいくらか。

(1)　€2,000 増加

(2)　€4,000 増加

(3)　€3,000 減少

(4)　€1,000 減少

(5)　上記のいずれでもない

解答　(1)

1-9

和訳 $7,000の機械を$4,000の現金で購入し差額は未払金とした。この取引の会計等式における影響は次のいずれか。

	資産	負債	資本
(1)	+ 7,000	+ 3,000	− 4,000
(2)	+ 7,000	− 4,000 ; − 3,000	増減なし
(3)	+ 4,000	− 4,000	増減なし
(4)	+ 7,000 ; − 4,000	+ 3,000	増減なし
(5)	上記のいずれでもない		

解答 (4)

解説 機械の増加は資産の増加、現金の支出は資産の減少、未払金の増加は負債の増加である。+ 7,000 + (− 4,000) = + 3,000 の等式が成り立つ。

1-10

和訳 C社の資産が $300,000、資本が $200,000 とすると、負債はいくらか。

(1) $500,000
(2) $300,000
(3) $200,000
(4) $100,000
(5) 上記のいずれでもない。

解答 (4)

解説 会計等式により、

Assets = Liabilities + Equity
Liabilities = Assets − Equity
= $300,000 − $200,000 = $100,000

1-11

和訳 D 社は 4 月に次の取引を行った。D 社の正しい現金 T- 勘定はどれか。

a．Y 氏が 4 月 1 日、$30,000 を出資して D 社を設立した。

b．D 社は 4 月 10 日、賃料を $10,000 支払った。

c．D 社は 1 月 20 日、給与を $5,000 支払った。

(1)

現金	
4/1　30,000	
4/10　10,000	
4/20　5,000	

(2)

現金	
	4/1　30,000
	4/10　10,000
	4/20　5,000

(3)

現金	
4/10　10,000	4/1　30,000
4/20　5,000	

(4)

現金	
4/20　5,000	4/1　30,000
	4/10　10,000

(5)

現金	
4/1　30,000	4/10　10,000
	4/20　5,000

解答 （5）

解説 それぞれの仕訳は以下の通り。

a．Cash　　　　　　　　30,000

　　　Share capital　　　　　　30,000

b．Rent expense　　　10,000

　　　Cash　　　　　　　　　10,000

c．Salaries expense　　5,000

　　　Cash　　　　　　　　　5,000

1-12

和訳 以下の勘定科目のうち、資産に該当するのはどれか。

(1) 現金

(2) 資本金

(3) 利益剰余金

(4) 買掛金

(5) 受取利息

解答 (1)

1-13

和訳 ABC社の負債は $300,000 で資本は$180,000である。ABC社の資産はいくらか。

(1) $120,000

(2) $150,000

(3) $180,000

(4) $300,000

(5) $480,000

解答 (5)

解説 $300,000 + $180,000 = $480,000

1-14

和訳 次の勘定を資産・負債・資本・収益・費用に分類しなさい。

(1) 設備

(2) 売上

(3) 給料

(4) 売掛金

(5) 支払手形

解答 (1) Assets

(2) Income

(3) Expenses

(4) Assets

(5) Liabilities

1-15

和訳　次の取引を T 勘定に記入しなさい。

(a) マイヤー氏は自分の会社を始めるにあたって、現金€20,000 を出資し、会社は同額の普通株式を発行した。

解答：

Cash				Share Capital	
20,000					20,000

(b) ABC 社は現金で€4,000 の設備を購入した。

解答：

Cash				Equipment	
	4,000			4,000	

(c) XYZ 社は水道光熱費€300 を現金で支払った。

解答：

Cash				Utilities Expense	
	300			300	

CHAPTER 2 —取引と仕訳—

Transactions and
Journal Entries

Bookkeeping & Accounting Test for International Communication

BATIC

2-1

和訳 スター社は旅費代金として旅行代理店に $200 支払った。次の仕訳のうち正しいものはどれか。

(1) 現金　　　　　　　　　200

　　　旅費　　　　　　　　　　　　200

(2) 現金　　　　　　　　　200

　　　賃借料　　　　　　　　　　　200

(3) 社債　　　　　　　　　200

　　　現金　　　　　　　　　　　　200

(4) 旅費　　　　　　　　　200

　　　現金　　　　　　　　　　　　200

(5) 上記のいずれでもない。

解答 (4)

2-2

和訳 次の取引を T 勘定に記入しなさい。

　　　7 月 5 日　当月の賃借料€250 を支払った。

　　　　　14 日　事務用の文房具購入のため現金€3 を支払った。

　　　　　19 日　切手購入のため現金€2 を支払った。

解答

2-3

和訳　テリー社は商品を掛けで $500 購入した。次のうち、正しい仕訳はどれか。

(1) 仕入　　　　　　　　　500

　　　　買掛金　　　　　　　　　　500

(2) 現金　　　　　　　　　500

　　　　仕入　　　　　　　　　　　500

(3) 売掛金　　　　　　　　500

　　　　現金　　　　　　　　　　　500

(4) 仕入　　　　　　　　　500

　　　　現金　　　　　　　　　　　500

(5) 買掛金　　　　　　　　500

　　　　仕入　　　　　　　　　　　500

解答　(1)

2-4

和訳　次の取引を T 勘定に記入しなさい。

2 月 3 日　商品 $300 を掛けで販売した。

解答

Accounts Receivable		Sales	
Feb. 3　300			Feb. 3　300

2-5

和訳 次の取引を T 勘定に記入しなさい。

2 月 3 日　R. Smith に商品 $300 を掛けで販売した。

11 日　R. Smith から売掛金のうち $100 を現金で回収した。

18 日　R. Smith から残りの $200 を現金で回収した。

解答

Accounts Receivable		Cash		Sales	
Feb. 3　300	Feb. 11 100	Feb. 11 100			Feb. 3　300
	18 200	18 200			

2-6

和訳 掛けで販売した商品€50が返品された。この取引に関して、販売側が記録すべき仕訳は次のうちどれか。販売者は返品に対して売上返品勘定を使用している。

(1) 売上　　　　　　　50

　　　現金　　　　　　　　　　50

(2) 売上返品　　　　　50

　　　現金　　　　　　　　　　50

(3) 売上　　　　　　　50

　　　売掛金　　　　　　　　　50

(4) 売上返品　　　　　50

　　　売掛金　　　　　　　　　50

(5) 上記のいずれでもない。

解答　(4)

2-7

和訳　2月5日にC社は商品 $1,000 を売上割引条件（受領後10日以内の支払いの場合は 2% の割引）で販売した。

購入者が2月6日に代金を支払う場合、いくら支払ったらよいか。

(1) $1,000

(2) $ 980

(3) $ 998

(4) $ 20

(5) $0

解答　(2)

2-8

和訳　20X0年12月1日、A社はB社に商品 $1,000 を売上割引条件（受領後10日以内の支払いの場合は 2% の割引）で販売した。B社は 20X0年12月12日に全額支払った。

売上割引額はいくらになるか。

(1) $1,000

(2) $ 200

(3) $ 20

(4) $ 10

(5) $0

解答　(5)

解説　支払いが条件の期限を過ぎているので、売上割引はなし。

2-9

和訳　ノートン社は $400 を銀行から借り入れ、支払手形を振り出した。
この取引の仕訳をしなさい。

解答　Cash　　　　　　　　　　　　400
　　　　　Notes payable　　　　　　　　　400

2-10

和訳　ノートン社は上記の支払手形のうち€100 を返済した。
この取引の仕訳をしなさい。

解答　Notes payable　　　　　　　100
　　　　　Cash　　　　　　　　　　　　100

2-11

和訳　以下は受取手形の例である。

20X0 年 11 月 1 日

私 William Smith は、ABC 社から借り受けた $900 について、20X0 年 11 月 1 日より 20 日後に、年率 6% の利息を付してお支払いいたします。

William Smith

---

1 年を 360 日と仮定しなさい。

(a) この手形の振出人は誰か。

(b) この手形の受取人は誰か。

(c) この手形の支払満期日はいつか。

(d) この手形の満期日での支払額はいくらか。

解答　(a) William Smith

(b) ABC Company

(c) 20X0 年 11 月 21 日

(d) $900 + $900 × 6% × (20 ÷ 360) = $903

2-12

和訳　ケント社は貸付金の利息 $5 を受け取った。

この取引の仕訳をしなさい。

解答　Cash　　　　　　　　　　5

　　　　Interest income　　　　　　　5

2-13

和訳 SSS 社は額面 $20,000 の約束手形を 90 日満期、年利 10% で買掛金の支払いと
して債権者に発行した。仕訳 (a) と (b) を作成しなさい。1 年を 360 日と仮
定しなさい。

(a) 手形の発行

(b) 適切な利息を含めた手形の支払い

解答 (a) Accounts payable   20,000

           Notes payable   20,000

(b) Notes payable   20,000

     Interest expense   500

           Cash   20,500

2-14

和訳 A 社について以下の仕訳を行いなさい。

(a) 現金 $9,000 に対し普通株式を発行した。

(b) 事務用家具 $5,000 を掛けにより購入した。

(c) 受取利息 $1,500 を受領した。

(d) 事務用備品 $8,000 を現金により購入した。

(e) 給料 $600 を現金で支払った。

解答

(a)	Cash	9,000	
	Share capital		9,000
(b)	Office furniture	5,000	
	Accounts payable		5,000
(c)	Cash	1,500	
	Interest income		1,500
(d)	Office equipment	8,000	
	Cash		8,000
(e)	Salaries expense	600	
	Cash		600

2-15

和訳　B社について以下の仕訳を行いなさい。

(a) 創業のために現金 $20,000、棚卸資産 $1,500、家具 $10,000 および備品 $11,000 を資本投資した。

(b) 消耗品 $2,000 を掛けで購入した。

(c) 報酬 $3,000 を請求した。

(d) 現金 $6,000 を追加投資した。

(e) 未払金残高の半分を現金で支払った。

解答　(a) Cash　　　　　　　　　　　20,000

　　　　　 Inventory　　　　　　　　1,500

　　　　　 Furniture　　　　　　　 10,000

　　　　　 Equipment　　　　　　 11,000

　　　　　　　 Share capital　　　　　　　　 42,500

　　　 (b) Supplies　　　　　　　　2,000

　　　　　　　 Accounts payable　　　　　　 2,000

　　　 (c) Accounts receivable　3,000

　　　　　　　 Fees income　　　　　　　　　 3,000

　　　 (d) Cash　　　　　　　　　　 6,000

　　　　　　　 Share capital　　　　　　　　　6,000

　　　 (e) Accounts payable　　 1,000

　　　　　　　 Cash　　　　　　　　　　　　 1,000

2-16

和訳 A 社は掛けで商品を売った。正しい仕訳を示しなさい。

(1) 借方　売上、貸方　現金

(2) 借方　現金、貸方　売上

(3) 借方　売上、貸方　売掛金

(4) 借方　売掛金、貸方　売上

(5) 上記のいずれでもない

解答 (4)

2-17

和訳 F 社は従業員の給料を支払った。正しい仕訳を示しなさい。

(1) 借方　現金、貸方　従業員

(2) 借方　現金、貸方　給料

(3) 借方　給料、貸方　現金

(4) 借方　従業員、貸方　現金

(5) 上記のいずれでもない

解答 (3)

2-18

和訳　以下の勘定は ABC 社の取引を示している。

該当する記述を選びなさい。

現金		手数料収入	
100			100

(1) 私用目的で会社の預金を引き出した。

(2) 給料を支払った。

(3) 銀行から借金をした。

(4) 自社に現金を投資した。

(5) 上記のいずれでもない。

解答　(5)

解説　役務に対する報酬を現金で受け取ったことを示している。よって、(5) 上記のいずれでもない が正解となる。

2-19

和訳　次の情報に基づき純仕入の金額を求めなさい。

仕入	$12,500
仕入運賃	1,500
仕入返品	2,100

解答　$11,900

解説　$12,500 + $1,500 − $2,100 = $11,900

2-20

和訳 ABC 社は 4 月 5 日に€2,000 の商品を 30 日以内 4% 割引の条件で販売した。購入者は 4 月 20 日に支払った。ABC 社は 4 月 20 日には次のどの仕訳を行うべきか。

(1) 現金　　　　　80
　　　売上　　　　　　　80

(2) 現金　　　　　80
　　　売上割引　　　　　80

(3) 現金　　　1,920
　　売上割引　　80
　　　売掛金　　　　　2,000

(4) 売上　　　　　80
　　　現金　　　　　　　80

(5) 売上割引　　　80
　　　売掛金　　　　　　80

解答　(3)

2-21

和訳 ABC 社は 4 月 5 日に $1,000 の商品を 20 日以内 3% 割引の条件で購入した。

(a) 4 月 10 日に支払うとしたら、ABC 社はいくら支払うべきか。

    (1) $0

    (2) $ 30

    (3) $ 833

    (4) $ 970

    (5) $1,000

解答：(4)

解説：$1,000 − $1,000 × 3% = $970

(b) 4 月 30 日に支払うとしたら、ABC 社はいくら支払うべきか。

    (1) $0

    (2) $ 30

    (3) $ 833

    (4) $ 970

    (5) $1,000

解答：(5)

解説：期限を過ぎているので、割引は適用されない。

2-22

和訳 XYZ 社は 10 月 1 日に現金 $50,000 で商品を販売した。顧客が破損した商品
を返品してきたので、現金 $150 を 10 月 20 日に返金した。

(a) XYZ 社は 10 月 1 日には次のどの仕訳を行うべきか。

(1) 売掛金　　　　　50,000

　　　売上　　　　　　　　　50,000

(2) 現金　　　　　　50,000

　　　売掛金　　　　　　　　50,000

(3) 現金　　　　　　50,000

　　　売上　　　　　　　　　50,000

(4) 売上　　　　　　50,000

　　　売掛金　　　　　　　　50,000

(5) 売上　　　　　　50,000

　　　現金　　　　　　　　　50,000

解答：(3)

(b) XYZ 社は 10 月 20 日には次のどの仕訳を行うべきか。

(1) 売上　　　　　　150

　　　売掛金　　　　　　　　150

(2) 売上　　　　　　150

　　　売上返品　　　　　　　150

(3) 売上返品　　　　150

　　　売掛金　　　　　　　　150

(4) 売上返品　　　　150

　　　現金　　　　　　　　　150

(5) 売上返品　　　　150

　　　売上　　　　　　　　　150

解答：(4)

2-23

和訳 XYZ 社は、買掛金の決済として、€10,000 の 30 日手形を額面で発行した。
手形の金利は 9.0% だった。

(a) XYZ 社が手形を発行したとき、次のどの仕訳を行うべきか。

(1) 買掛金   10,000

    支払手形   10,000

(2) 現金   10,000

    支払手形   10,000

(3) 支払手形   10,000

    買掛金   10,000

(4) 受取手形   10,000

    売掛金   10,000

(5) 受取手形   10,000

    現金   10,000

解答：(1)

(b) XYZ 社が手形を決済したとき、次のどの仕訳を行うべきか。1年を360
日と仮定しなさい。

(1) 現金　　　　　　　10,075

　　　支払手形　　　　　　　　　10,000
　　　支払利息　　　　　　　　　　　75

(2) 現金　　　　　　　10,900

　　　支払手形　　　　　　　　　10,000
　　　支払利息　　　　　　　　　900

(3) 支払手形　　　　　10,000

　　　現金　　　　　　　　　　　10,000

(4) 支払手形　　　　　10,000

　　支払利息　　　　　　75

　　　現金　　　　　　　　　　　10,075

(5) 支払手形　　　　　10,000

　　支払利息　　　　　900

　　　現金　　　　　　　　　　　10,900

解答：(4)

解説：Interest expense（支払利息）の計算 = €10,000×9%×30 日/360 日 = €75

Journal and Ledger

3-1

和訳 次の取引を一般仕訳帳に記入し、それから元帳に転記しなさい。

20X0 年

4 月 3 日　€275 の商品を掛けで購入した。

　　　5 日　€800 の商品を現金で販売した。

　　　10 日　€320 の商品を現金で購入した。

　　　18 日　€700 の商品を掛けで販売した。

解答

	General Journal				J3
Date	Account and Explanation		P.R.	Debit	Credit
20X0					
Apr. 3	Purchases		501	275	
		Accounts payable	201		275
5	Cash		101	800	
		Sales	401		800
10	Purchases		501	320	
		Cash	101		320
18	Accounts receivable		102	700	
		Sales	401		700

General Ledger

	Cash				101
Date	Explanation	P.R.	Debit	Credit	Balance
20X0					
Apr. 5		J3	800		800
10		J3		320	480

	Accounts Receivable				102
Date	Explanation	P.R.	Debit	Credit	Balance
20X0					
Apr. 18		J3	700		700

	Accounts Payable				201
Date	Explanation	P.R.	Debit	Credit	Balance
20X0					
Apr. 3		J3		275	275

Sales   401

Date	Explanation	P.R.	Debit	Credit	Balance
20X0					
Apr. 5		J3		800	800
18		J3		700	1,500

Purchases   501

Date	Explanation	P.R.	Debit	Credit	Balance
20X0					
Apr. 3		J3	275		275
10		J3	320		595

Chapter 3

171

3-2

和訳　ABC 社は 20X0 年 5 月中に次の取引を行った。

| 日付 | 取引 |

5 月 2 日　€10,000 相当の設備の出資に対し、同額の普通株式を発行した。

6 日　€2,500 の商品を掛けで購入した。

10 日　€3,000 の商品を現金で販売した。

14 日　€30 の事務用消耗品を現金で購入した。

19 日　€1,800 の商品を掛けで販売した。

22 日　買掛金の決済で現金€2,000 を支払った。

28 日　売掛金の決済で現金€600 を受け取った。

次の取引を一般仕訳帳に記入し、それから元帳に転記しなさい。

解答

General Journal				J4
Date	Account and Explanation	P.R.	Debit	Credit
20X0				
May 2	Equipment	110	10,000	
	Share capital	301		10,000
6	Purchases	501	2,500	
	Accounts payable	201		2,500
10	Cash	101	3,000	
	Sales	401		3,000
14	Office supplies expense	508	30	
	Cash	101		30
19	Accounts receivable	102	1,800	
	Sales	401		1,800
22	Account payable	201	2,000	
	Cash	101		2,000
28	Cash	101	600	
	Account receivable	102		600

General Ledger

Cash 101

Date	Explanation	P.R.	Debit	Credit	Balance
20X0					
May 10		J4	3,000		3,000
14		J4		30	2,970
22		J4		2,000	970
28		J4	600		1,570

Accounts Receivable 102

Date	Explanation	P.R.	Debit	Credit	Balance
20X0					
May 19		J4	1,800		1,800
28		J4		600	1,200

Equipment 110

Date	Explanation	P.R.	Debit	Credit	Balance
20X0					
May 2		J4	10,000		10,000

Accounts Payable 201

Date	Explanation	P.R.	Debit	Credit	Balance
20X0					
May 6		J4		2,500	2,500
22		J4	2,000		500

Share Capital 301

Date	Explanation	P.R.	Debit	Credit	Balance
20X0					
May 2		J4		10,000	10,000

Sales 401

Date	Explanation	P.R.	Debit	Credit	Balance
20X0					
May 10		J4		3,000	3,000
19		J4		1,800	4,800

Chapter 3

Purchases 501

Date	Explanation	P.R.	Debit	Credit	Balance
20X0					
May 6		J4	2,500		2,500

Office Supplies Expense 508

Date	Explanation	P.R.	Debit	Credit	Balance
20X0					
May 14		J4	30		30

解答編

CHAPTER 4 —試算表—

Trial Balance

Bookkeeping & Accounting Test for International Communication

BATIC

4-1

和訳 試算表の作成によって発見することができるエラーは次のうちのどれか。

(1) 取引の記帳もれ

(2) 貸借一方の仕訳または、貸借の金額が異なる仕訳

(3) 二重仕訳または、重複転記

(4) 誤った勘定科目への転記

(5) 上記全て

解答 (2)

解説 Trial balance（試算表）によって検証できるエラーは、結果として貸借が不一致となるもののみである。よって、Double journalizing（二重仕訳）など貸借が一致してしまうエラーは、発見できない。

4-2

和訳　ABC 社の試算表は以下のとおりである。

いくつかの勘定について、元帳から試算表に数字を転記する際にミスがあったため、残高が合わなくなっている。各勘定について、通常の貸借の残高に訂正し、正しい試算表を作成しなさい。

ABC 社
試算表
20X0 年 1 月 31 日

	借方	貸方
現金	$32,000	
売掛金		$ 5,000
買掛金	3,000	
資本金		14,000
売上	28,000	
消耗品費	1,000	
給料	3,000	
販売費		4,000
合計	$67,000	$23,000

解答

ABC Company
Trial Balance
January 31, 20X0

	Dr.	Cr.
Cash	$32,000	
Accounts Receivable	5,000	
Accounts Payable		$ 3,000
Share Capital		14,000
Sales		28,000
Supplies Expense	1,000	
Salaries Expense	3,000	
Sales Expense	4,000	
Total	$45,000	$45,000

4-3

和訳 ABC 社の 12 月の財務情報は以下のとおりである。

12 月　1 日　現金 $13,000、備品 $5,000 を出資して事業を始めた。

　　　 3 日　追加の備品 $3,000 を掛けで購入した。

　　　 7 日　消耗品 $1,600 を現金で購入した。

　　　12 日　買掛金を $1,500 返済した。

　　　16 日　当月中に稼いだ報酬 $3,400 を受け取った。

　　　23 日　臨時アシスタントの給料 $400 を支払った。

　　　28 日　備品の買掛金の残りを返済した。

各取引を以下の T 勘定に記入しなさい。

解答

	Cash						Supplies		
Dec.	1	13,000	Dec.	7	1,600	Dec.	7	1,600	
	16	3,400		12	1,500				
				23	400		Equipment		
				28	1,500	Dec.	1	5,000	
							3	3,000	

	Accounts Payable						Share Capital		
Dec.	12	1,500	Dec.	3	3,000			Dec.	1	18,000
	28	1,500							

	Fees Income						Salaries Expense		
			Dec.	16	3,400	Dec.	23	400	

4-4

和訳 前述の情報をもとに試算表を作成しなさい。

解答

ABC Company
Trial Balance
December 31, 20X0

	Dr.	Cr.
Cash	$11,400	
Supplies	1,600	
Equipment	8,000	
Share Capital		$18,000
Fees Income		3,400
Salaries Expense	400	
Total	$21,400	$21,400

4-5

和訳 次の取引を T 勘定に記入しなさい。

5月 1日 M. Owen 氏は現金 $5,000 を出資して、事業を開始した。

4日 消耗品 $400 を現金で購入した。

5日 ABC 社から家具 $3,000 を掛けで購入した。

15日 当月中に稼いだ報酬 $3,500 を受け取った。

30日 臨時アシスタントの給料 $300 を支払った。

30日 5月分の事務所賃借料 $1,500 を支払った。

31日 ABC 社に未払金のうち $2,200 を返済した。

解答

	Cash				
May 1	5,000	May 4	400
15	3,500	30	300
		30	1,500
		31	2,200

	Supplies		
May 4	400		

	Furniture		
May 5	3,000		

	Accounts Payable			
May 31	2,200	May 5	3,000

	Share Capital		
		May 1	5,000

	Fees Income		
		May 15	3,500

	Rent Expense		
May 30	1,500		

	Salaries Expense		
May 30	300		

4-6

和訳　前述の情報をもとに、試算表を作成しなさい。

解答

M. Owen
Trial Balance
May 31, 20X0

	Dr.	Cr.
Cash	$4,100	
Supplies	400	
Furniture	3,000	
Accounts Payable		$ 800
Share Capital		5,000
Fees Income		3,500
Rent Expense	1,500	
Salaries Expense	300	
Total	$9,300	$9,300

4-7

和訳　次のうち試算表において発見できない誤りはどれか。

(1) 買掛金残高€400 が試算表から漏れていた。

(2) €700 の商品の購入を含む取引が計上されなかった。

(3) €1,000 の未払費用が試算表において借方に計上されていた。

(4) €800 の売上高が漏れていた。

(5) 上記のいずれでもない。

解答　(2)

解説　試算表の貸借の不一致によって発見される誤りもあるが、貸借が一致するような誤りは発見されない。例えば、貸借の金額は正しいが、勘定科目が間違っている場合、貸借ともに同額で誤った金額であった場合、あるいは取引そのものの記録が完全に抜けていた場合である。

Chapter 4

4-8

和訳 マーク・クリーニングの 20X0 年 7 月 31 日の試算表は次の通りである。

マーク・クリーニング
試算表
20X0 年 7 月 31 日

現金	$10,000	
売掛金	20,000	
家具	700	
備品	1,500	
未払金		$ 8,800
支払手形		10,400
資本金		10,000
利益剰余金		3,000
	$32,200	$32,200

8 月の取引は次の通りである。

8 月 3 日　未払金 $1,800 を支払った。

9 日　支払手形 $1,000 を支払った。

13 日　クリーニング代として $8,000 受け取った。

22 日　備品を $20,000 で購入し、頭金を $7,000 支払った。

25 日　専門家への手数料を $2,000 支払った。

31 日　現金 $5,000 の追加投資を行った。

この情報を使って 20X0 年 8 月 31 日の試算表を作成しなさい。

解答

Mark Cleaning
Trial Balance
August 31, 20X0

Cash	$11,200	
Accounts Receivable	20,000	
Furniture	700	
Equipment	21,500	
Accounts Payable		$20,000
Notes Payable		9,400
Share Capital		15,000
Retained Earnings		3,000
Cleaning Income		8,000
Professional Fees	2,000	
	$55,400	$55,400

Chapter 4

4-9

和訳　次を使って 20X0 年 12 月 31 日の D 社の試算表を作成しなさい。

現金	$ 9,400
売掛金	1,000
消耗品	700
備品	900
建物	11,000
買掛金	10,000
資本金	5,000
利益剰余金	1,000
配送収入	12,000
支払保険料	3,000
専門家への支払手数料	2,000

解答

D Company
Trial Balance
December 31, 20X0

Cash	$ 9,400	
Accounts Receivable	1,000	
Supplies	700	
Equipment	900	
Building	11,000	
Accounts Payable		$10,000
Share Capital		5,000
Retained Earnings		1,000
Income from Delivery		12,000
Insurance Expense	3,000	
Professional Fees	2,000	
	$28,000	$28,000

4-10

和訳 E 社の仕訳を下記の T 勘定に転記しなさい。

(a) 現金　　　　　　　　　　8,000

　　　資本金　　　　　　　　　　　　8,000

(b) 事務用消耗品　　　　　　3,000

　　　未払金　　　　　　　　　　　　2,000

　　　現金　　　　　　　　　　　　　1,000

(c) 売掛金　　　　　　　　　500

　　　クリーニング収入　　　　　　　500

(d) 家賃　　　　　　　　　　800

　　　現金　　　　　　　　　　　　　800

(e) 未払金　　　　　　　　1,000

　　　現金　　　　　　　　　　　　1,000

解答

Cash			
(a)	8,000	(b)	1,000
		(d)	800
		(e)	1,000

Accounts Receivable	
(c) 500	

Office Supplies	
(b) 3,000	

Accounts Payable			
(e)	1,000	(b)	2,000

Share Capital	
	(a) 8,000

Cleaning Income	
	(c) 500

Rent Expense	
(d) 800	

4-11

和訳 前述の勘定残高を使って試算表を作成しなさい。

解答

E Company
Trial Balance

Cash	$5,200	
Accounts Receivable	500	
Office Supplies	3,000	
Accounts Payable		$1,000
Share Capital		8,000
Cleaning Income		500
Rent Expense	800	
	$9,500	$9,500

4-12

和訳 次のステップを適切な順序に並べ替えなさい。

Ⅰ.試算表の作成

Ⅱ.総勘定元帳への転記

Ⅲ.取引の発生

Ⅳ.仕訳

(1) Ⅲ － Ⅱ － Ⅰ － Ⅳ

(2) Ⅲ － Ⅰ － Ⅳ － Ⅱ

(3) Ⅲ － Ⅳ － Ⅰ － Ⅱ

(4) Ⅲ － Ⅱ － Ⅳ － Ⅰ

(5) Ⅲ － Ⅳ － Ⅱ － Ⅰ

解答 (5)

解説 Double-entry system（複式簿記）の流れ

① Transaction（取引）が発生する。

② Journal entry（仕訳）を行う。

③ Journal から General ledger へ転記する。

④ 月末において、各 Accounts の残高の正確性を検証するため、Trial balance（試算表）を作成する。

Chapter 4

4-13

和訳 次の情報は ABC 社の 20X0 年 6 月 30 日の勘定に関するものである。

現金	?
売掛金	2,100
土地	10,000
買掛金	2,500
資本金	20,000
利益剰余金	8,000
売上	19,000
仕入	16,000
給料	10,000

現金の金額を計算し、ABC の試算表を作成しなさい。合計欄以外、金額は借方・貸方のいずれかに記入し、相手側は未記入とすること。

解答

		($)
Account Title	Dr.	Cr.
Cash	11,400	
Accounts receivable	2,100	
Land	10,000	
Accounts payable		2,500
Share capital		20,000
Retained earnings		8,000
Sales		19,000
Purchases	16,000	
Salaries expense	10,000	
Total	49,500	49,500

4-14

和訳 前述のケースで、次の取引が記録されていなかったと仮定しなさい。

日付	取引
5	$5,500 の商品を掛けで購入した。
7	売掛金の決済として現金 $1,000 を受け取った。
11	商品を販売し、現金 $8,000 を受け取った。
20	給料として、現金 $2,000 を支払った。

解答

		($)
Account Title	Dr.	Cr.
Cash	18,400	
Accounts receivable	1,100	
Land	10,000	
Accounts payable		8,000
Share capital		20,000
Retained earnings		8,000
Sales		27,000
Purchases	21,500	
Salaries expense	12,000	
Total	63,000	63,000

解説 追加の仕訳は以下のとおり。

5日	Purchases	5,500	
	Accounts payable		5,500
7日	Cash	1,000	
	Accounts receivable		1,000
11日	Cash	8,000	
	Sales		8,000
20日	Salaries expense	2,000	
	Cash		2,000

4-15

和訳　20X2 年 6 月 30 日、キッテル社の月次試算表の貸借が一致しなかった。

キッテル社
試算表
20X2 年 6 月 30 日

(€)

	借方	貸方
現金	5,200	
売掛金	3,600	
買掛金		5,300
資本金		2,000
利益剰余金		500
売上		19,000
給料	13,100	
賃借料	5,000	
	26,900	26,800

元帳と仕訳帳を見直したところ、以下の誤りが明らかになった。

・水道光熱費€1,000 の支払いが、賃借料勘定の借方に記帳された。

・売掛金の回収€600 が、現金勘定の借方に€800、買掛金勘定の貸方に€800 記帳された。

・給与€200 の支払いの仕訳が、給与勘定の借方に€300 記帳された。

修正した試算表を作成しなさい。

解答

Kittel Company
Trial balance
June 30, 20X2

(€)

	Dr.	Cr.
Cash	5,000	
Accounts receivable	3,000	
Accounts payable		4,500
Share capital		2,000
Retained earnings		500
Sales		19,000
Salaries expense	13,000	
Rent expense	4,000	
Utilities expense	1,000	
	26,000	26,000

Adjusting Entries

Bookkeeping & Accounting Test for International Communication

BATIC

5-1

和訳 次の仕訳をT勘定に転記しなさい。

<table>
<tr><th colspan="4" style="text-align:center">一般仕訳帳</th><th>G4</th></tr>
<tr><th>Date</th><th>Accounts</th><th>Dr.</th><th>Cr.</th></tr>
<tr><td>2月11日</td><td>現金</td><td>170</td><td></td></tr>
<tr><td></td><td>　売掛金</td><td></td><td>170</td></tr>
<tr><td>14日</td><td>売掛金</td><td>500</td><td></td></tr>
<tr><td></td><td>　売上</td><td></td><td>500</td></tr>
<tr><td>17日</td><td>家賃</td><td>300</td><td></td></tr>
<tr><td></td><td>　未払家賃</td><td></td><td>300</td></tr>
<tr><td>28日</td><td>未払家賃</td><td>150</td><td></td></tr>
<tr><td></td><td>　現金</td><td></td><td>150</td></tr>
<tr><td>29日</td><td>減価償却費</td><td>20</td><td></td></tr>
<tr><td></td><td>　減価償却累計額</td><td></td><td>20</td></tr>
</table>

解答

Cash		Accounts Receivable		Accumulated Depreciation	
2/11 G4* 170	2/28 G4 * 150	2/14 G4 * 500	2/11 G4 * 170		2/29 G4 * 20

Rent Payable		Sales		Rent	
2/28 G4 * 150	2/17 G4 * 300		2/14 G4 * 500	2/17 G4 * 300	

Depreciation Expense	
2/29 G4 * 20	

＊ G4 はなくても正解とする。

5-2

和訳 サービス報酬を前もって受け取った。これは次の3年間にわたって提供されるサービスに対するものである。受け取った報酬はいつ収益に認識されるべきか。

(1) 報酬を受け取る期間
(2) サービスを提供する期間
(3) サービスが始まる日
(4) サービスが終わる日
(5) 上記のいずれでもない

解答 (2)

解説 発生主義会計において、会計事実の認識は入金などの時点に囚われずにその取引が発生した時点で行うというものである。従って、サービスを提供する3年間にわたり収益を計上する。

5-3

和訳 20X0年11月1日、キー社は3年の保険契約の保険料$3,600を支払った。20X0年12月31日の財務諸表にいくら支払保険料として計上すべきか。

(1) $3,600
(2) $ 200
(3) $0
(4) $1,200
(5) 上記のいずれでもない

解答 (2)

解説 20X0年11月1日から3年間の保険料として$3,600を支払ったので、12月31日までの保険料は2/36ヶ月で、$200である。

5-4

和訳 チャイナ社は種々の契約によって特許権のいくつかを他の会社に使用許諾している。特許権のロイヤルティは契約締結時に受領するものと、期間終了後ごとに受領するものがある。以下のデータはチャイナ社の各期の12月31日現在の貸借対照表のものである。

	20X1	20X2
未収ロイヤルティ	$80,000	$90,000
前受ロイヤルティ	45,000	50,000

20X2年中にチャイナ社は$250,000のロイヤルティの送金を受けた。20X2年12月31日の損益計算書において、チャイナ社はロイヤルティ収益にいくら計上すべきか。

(1) $200,000

(2) $210,000

(3) $235,000

(4) $255,000

(5) 上記のいずれでもない

解答 (4)

解説 20X2年度に回収されたロイヤルティ$250,000のうち、期首の未収ロイヤルティ残高$80,000は20X1年度の収益としてすでに認識されているため、20X2年度の収益には含まれない。20X2年度期末の未収ロイヤルティ残高$90,000はまだ回収はされていないが、20X2年度の収益として認識される。期首の前受ロイヤルティ残高$45,000は、入金は前期にあるが今期の収益となり、また、期末の前受ロイヤルティ残高は今期の収益とはならず、翌期の収益となる。

20X2 cash received	$250,000
Royalty receivable 12/31/20X1	(80,000)
Royalty receivable 12/31/20X2	90,000
Unearned royalty 12/31/20X1	45,000
Unearned royalty 12/31/20X2	(50,000)
Royalty income	$255,000

| 5-5 |

和訳 ブルー社は20X0年7月1日に新しい工場を€700,000で取得した。その見積
耐用年数は20年であり、残存価額は€60,000であった。ブルー社の会計期間
は暦年である。ブルー社は減価償却に定額法を使用している。20X0年の損
益計算書においてブルー社はこの工場に対しいくらの減価償却費を計上しな
ければならないか。

(1) €0

(2) €16,000

(3) €32,000

(4) €35,000

(5) 上記のいずれでもない

解答 (2)

解説 定額法の計算式は

減価償却費 =（取得価額 − 残存価額）÷ 耐用年数　であるので、

（€700,000 − €60,000）÷20 = €32,000

今回は取得が期中であるため、月割計算を行うので、

€32,000×6/12 = €16,000

5-6

和訳 アンジェラ社は 20X1 年 7 月 1 日に $10,000 で設備を取得した。
その設備の耐用年数は 5 年、残存価額は $1,200 と見積もられている。
アンジェラ社は 2 倍定率法を使用している。20X2 年 12 月 31 日現在の貸借
対照表において減価償却累計額はいくら計上すべきか。

(1) $2,640

(2) $4,576

(3) $5,200

(4) $5,280

(5) 上記のいずれでもない

解答 (3)

解説 2 倍定率法の計算式は

減価償却費 = 取得価額 × 定額法償却率 × 2

また 20X1 年分は月割りが必要である。

よって 20X1 年分 = $10,000 × 40% × 6/12 = $2,000

20X2 年分 = ($10,000 − $2,000) × 40% = $3,200

$2,000 + $3,200 = $5,200

5-7

和訳 20X0 年 10 月 1 日に 4 年の賃貸契約が結ばれ、$2,400 が支払われた。これは
前払家賃として借方に記録された。20X0 年 12 月 31 日期末の修正仕訳を行
いなさい。

解答 Rent expense   150

Prepaid rent   150

解説 $2,400 ÷ 4 × 3/12 = $150

5-8

和訳 ABC社は20X0年1月1日に原価$45,000、耐用年数10年、残存価額$3,000
の資産を取得した。

級数法を使用した20X0年度の減価償却費はいくらか。

(1) $4,250

(2) $4,500

(3) $8,181

(4) $9,000

(5) 上記のいずれでもない

解答 (5)

解説 ($45,000 − $3,000) × 10 ÷ 55 = $7,636

$55 = 1 + 2 + 3 + \cdots \cdots + 10 = 10 \times ((10 + 1)/2)$

5-9

和訳 事務用消耗品$1,500は事務用消耗品(資産勘定)として借方に記帳された。
期末には$600手元に残っていた。

(a) 修正仕訳を行いなさい。

(b) 購入時に消耗品費として借方記帳されていた場合の修正仕訳を行い
なさい。

解答
(a) Office supplies expense	900	
Office supplies		900
(b) Office supplies	600	
Office supplies expense		600

5-10

和訳 1週間分の賃金$1,000（1週は5日）が金曜日に支払われる。火曜日に終わる
事業年度の修正仕訳の金額はいくらか。

(1) $1,000

(2) $ 600

(3) $ 400

(4) $0

(5) 上記のいずれでもない

解答 (3)

解説 $1,000÷5 days = $200 per day

$200×2 days = $400

Salaries expense   400

　　　Salaries payable   400

5-11

和訳 12月31日の消耗品勘定の修正前残高は $1,200 であった。期末の棚卸では $400 が手元にあった。修正仕訳の金額はいくらか。

(1) $ 400

(2) $ 800

(3) $1,200

(4) $1,600

(5) 上記のいずれでもない

解答 (2)

解説 $1,200 - $400 = $800

Supplies expense	800	
Supplies		800

5-12

和訳　次のうち備品の減価償却を計上する修正仕訳として正しいのはどれか。

(1) 借方　減価償却費　　　　　　貸方　未払金

(2) 借方　減価償却費　　　　　　貸方　減価償却累計額

(3) 借方　減価償却累計額　　　　貸方　備品

(4) 借方　未払金　　　　　　　　貸方　減価償却費

(5) 上記のいずれでもない

解答　(2)

5-13

和訳　次のうち年末時点で、支払い義務はあるが未払いの給料の修正仕訳として正しいのはどれか。

(1) 借方　未払給料　　　　　　　貸方　給料

(2) 借方　現金　　　　　　　　　貸方　給料

(3) 借方　給料　　　　　　　　　貸方　未払給料

(4) 修正仕訳は必要ない

(5) 上記のいずれでもない

解答　(3)

5-14

和訳 20X1年12月31日期の期首の前払保険料の残高は$1,600であった。保険料
1年分$3,200が20X0年7月1日に支払われている。20X1年7月1日には$2,000
の1年分保険料が支払われた。20X1年12月31日の貸借対照表における前
払保険料はいくらになるか。

(1) $1,000

(2) $2,000

(3) $2,600

(4) $3,600

(5) 上記のいずれでもない

解答 (1)

解説 $2,000 \times 6/12 = \$1,000$

5-15

和訳 会計年度が暦年である ABC 社は、事務用消耗品€3,000を掛けで購入し、資産勘定に記帳した。年末には€400 が未使用で残っていた。

ABC 社が事務用消耗品を購入した際に、次のどの仕訳を行ったか。

(1) 事務用消耗品　　　　　　3,000
　　　現金　　　　　　　　　　　　　　3,000

(2) 事務用消耗品　　　　　　3,000
　　　未払金　　　　　　　　　　　　　3,000

(3) 現金　　　　　　　　　　3,000
　　　未払金　　　　　　　　　　　　　3,000

(4) 現金　　　　　　　　　　3,000
　　　事務用消耗品　　　　　　　　　　3,000

(5) 未払金　　　　　　　　　3,000
　　　事務用消耗品　　　　　　　　　　3,000

解答 (2)

5-16

和訳　前述のケースにおいて、ABC 社は年末に正しい決算修正仕訳を行った。資産、負債、資本に与える影響はどのようになるか。

	資産	負債	資本
(1)	減少	減少	影響なし
(2)	減少	影響なし	減少
(3)	影響なし	影響なし	影響なし
(4)	増加	増加	減少
(5)	増加	影響なし	増加

解答　(2)

5-17

和訳　3月1日に、会計年度が暦年である ABC 社は XYZ 社に事務所を貸し出し、$9,000の現金を年間の賃料として受け取った。ABC 社が最初の年に報告すべき賃貸料はいくらか。

解答　$7,500
解説　$9,000×10 ヵ月/12 ヵ月 = $7,500

5-18

和訳　会計年度が暦年である ABC 社は9月1日に銀行から$12,000を借りた。年利9%は毎年8月31日に支払い、3年後に元本を返済する予定である。最初の年に報告すべき支払利息はいくらか。1年を360日と仮定しなさい。

解答　$363
解説　$12,000×9% ×121 日/360 日 = $363　　※121 日 = 29 + 31 + 30 + 31

5-19

和訳　ABC 社は次の固定資産を保有している。

	取得日	取得原価	耐用年数	残存価額	減価償却方法
建物	20X3 年 1 月 1 日	$80,000	20 年	$10,000	定額法
機械装置	20X4 年 6 月 1 日	$50,000	5 年	$ 5,000	定額法
車両運搬具	20X5 年 1 月 1 日	$15,000	10 年	$ 2,000	2 倍定率法

ABC の会計年度は 12 月 31 日に終了する。

20X5 年の財務諸表において ABC 社が報告すべき次の金額を計算しなさい。

(a) 建物の減価償却費

(b) 建物の簿価

(c) 機械装置の減価償却累計額

(d) 車両運搬具の減価償却費

解答＆解説

(a) ($80,000 − $10,000)/20 年 = $3,500

(b) $80,000 − $3,500×3 年 = $69,500

(c) 年間の減価償却費は ($50,000 − $5,000)/5 年 = $9,000

　　したがって、減価償却累計額は $9,000×7 ヵ月/12 ヵ月 + $9,000 = $14,250

(d) 償却率 = 1/10×2 = 0.2 よって求める減価償却費は $15,000×0.2 = $3,000

5-20

和訳　A 社の試算表は次のとおりである。

($)

勘定科目	借方	貸方
現金	18,300	
売掛金	5,200	
建物	20,000	
買掛金		3,500
資本金		20,000
利益剰余金		9,000
売上		25,000
給料	14,000	
	57,500	57,500

決算整理仕訳に必要な情報は以下のとおりである。

・20X0 年の減価償却費は $2,000 であった。

・未払いの給料は $3,000 であった。

修正後残高試算表を完成させなさい。

解答

($)

Account Title	Trial Balance		Adjustment		Adjusted Trial Balance	
	Dr.	Cr.	Dr.	Cr.	Dr.	Cr.
Cash	18,300				18,300	
Accounts receivable	5,200				5,200	
Building	20,000				20,000	
(Accumulated depreciation)				2,000		2,000
Accounts payable		3,500				3,500
(Salaries payable)				3,000		3,000
Share capital		20,000				20,000
Retained earnings		9,000				9,000
Sales		25,000				25,000
Salaries expense	14,000		3,000		17,000	
(Depreciation expense)			2,000		2,000	
Total	57,500	57,500	5,000	5,000	62,500	62,500

5-21

和訳 11月1日、会計年度が暦年である ABC 社は、XYZ 社に $12,000 貸し付けた。
毎年10月31日に年利6%を受け取り、元本の支払いは3年後になっている。
ABC 社が最初の年度末に行うべき仕訳は次のうちどれか。1年を360日と
仮定しなさい。

(1) 現金　　　　　　　　120
　　　受取利息　　　　　　　　　120
(2) 現金　　　　　　　2,160
　　　受取利息　　　　　　　　2,160
(3) 未収利息　　　　　　120
　　　受取利息　　　　　　　　　120
(4) 未収利息　　　　　2,160
　　　受取利息　　　　　　　　2,160
(5) 仕訳は必要ない。

解答：(3)

解説： $12,000×6%×60日／360日 = $120
　　　※60日 = 29日 + 31日

5-22

和訳 ABC 社は次の固定資産を保有している。

	取得日	取得原価	耐用年数	残存価額	減価償却方法
建物	20X3 年 1 月 1 日	€100,000	10 年	€10,000	定額法
車両運搬具	20X4 年 1 月 1 日	€15,000	5 年	€1,500	2 倍定率法
オフィス設備	20X4 年 1 月 1 日	€120,000	10 年	€10,000	級数法

ABC の会計年度は 12 月 31 日に終了する。

20X5 年の財務諸表において ABC 社が報告すべき次の金額を計算しなさい。

(a) 建物の減価償却費

(b) 建物の簿価

(c) 車両運搬具の減価償却費

(d) 車両運搬具の減価償却累計額

(e) オフィス設備の減価償却費

解答＆解説：

(a) （€100,000 − €10,000）/10 年 = €9,000

(b) €100,000 − €9,000×3 年 = €73,000

(c) 償却率 = 1/5×2 = 0.4

　　20X4 年の減価償却費：€15,000×0.4 = €6,000

　　20X5 年の減価償却費：（€15,000 − €6,000）×0.4 = €3,600

(d) €6,000+€3,600 = €9,600

(e) 20X5 年の償却率 = 9/（10+9+⋯+1） = 9/55

　　よって求める減価償却費は （€120,000 − €10,000）×9/55 = €18,000

5-23

和訳 20X0年10月3日、会計年度が暦年であるABC社は、事務用消耗品$1,500を現金で購入し、費用勘定に記帳した。20X0年12月31日、$900が未使用で残っていた。

ABC社が再振替仕訳を行う場合、20X1年の期首に行うべき仕訳は次のうちどれか。

(1) 事務用消耗品　　　　　　600
　　　　事務用消耗品費　　　　　　600
(2) 事務用消耗品費　　　　　600
　　　　事務用消耗品　　　　　　　600
(3) 事務用消耗品　　　　　　900
　　　　事務用消耗品費　　　　　　900
(4) 事務用消耗品費　　　　　900
　　　　事務用消耗品　　　　　　　900
(5) 仕訳は必要ない。

解答 (4)

解説 20X0年10月3日の仕訳
事務用消耗品費　　　　　1,500
　　　現金　　　　　　　　　　1,500

20X0年12月31日の決算修正仕訳
事務用消耗品　　　　　900
　　　事務用消耗品費　　　　900

CHAPTER 6 　―棚卸資産と売上原価の会計処理―

Accounting for Inventory and Cost of Sales

Bookkeeping & Accounting Test for International Communication

BATIC

6-1

和訳 次の情報から売上原価をもとめなさい。

期首商品棚卸高	$5,000
当期商品仕入高	$3,700
期末商品棚卸高	$2,500

(1) $2,500

(2) $3,700

(3) $5,000

(4) $6,200

(5) 上記のいずれでもない

解答 (4)

6-2

和訳 次の情報から売上原価をもとめなさい。

期首商品棚卸高	€ 2,000
当期商品仕入高	30,000
当期商品仕入割引高	4,000
当期仕入に係わる輸送費	1,000
期末商品棚卸高	3,000

(1) €24,000

(2) €26,000

(3) €27,000

(4) €29,000

(5) €30,000

解答 (2)

解説 仕入に係わる輸送費は売上原価に算入する。従って、純仕入高は

€30,000 − €4,000 + €1,000 = €27,000

売上原価は、€2,000 + €27,000 − €3,000 = €26,000

6-3

和訳 C社は商品を現金で購入した。棚卸計算法の下での正しい仕訳を示しなさい。

(1) 借方　商品、貸方　現金

(2) 借方　現金、貸方　仕入

(3) 借方　仕入、貸方　現金

(4) 借方　現金、貸方　商品

(5) 上記のいずれでもない

解答　(3)

6-4

和訳 ABC社は棚卸計算法を使っている。5月1日に、現金\$3,000で商品を購入し、6月30日にその商品を\$8,000で販売し現金を受け取った。

(a) 5月1日の仕訳を行いなさい。

解答

Purchases	3,000	
Cash		3,000

(b) 6月30日の仕訳を行いなさい。

解答

Cash	8,000	
Sales		8,000

6-5

和訳　継続記録法を使用している ABC 社は次のような取引があった。

日付	取引
8 月 3 日	商品€5,000 を掛けで仕入れた。
8 月 20 日	上記の商品を販売し、現金€11,000 を受け取った。

（a）ABC 社は 8 月 3 日には、次のどの仕訳を行うべきか。

（1）	棚卸資産	5,000	
	買掛金		5,000
（2）	棚卸資産	5,000	
	現金		5,000
（3）	棚卸資産	5,000	
	仕入		5,000
（4）	仕入	5,000	
	買掛金		5,000
（5）	仕入	5,000	
	現金		5,000

解答　（1）

(b) ABC 社は 8 月 20 日には、次のどの仕訳を行うべきか。

(1) 売掛金　　　　　　11,000
　　　　売上　　　　　　　　　　11,000
(2) 現金　　　　　　　11,000
　　　　売上　　　　　　　　　　11,000
(3) 売掛金　　　　　　11,000
　　棚卸資産　　　　　5,000
　　　　売上　　　　　　　　　　11,000
　　　　売上原価　　　　　　　　5,000
(4) 現金　　　　　　　11,000
　　棚卸資産　　　　　5,000
　　　　売上　　　　　　　　　　11,000
　　　　仕入　　　　　　　　　　5,000
(5) 現金　　　　　　　11,000
　　売上原価　　　　　5,000
　　　　売上　　　　　　　　　　11,000
　　　　棚卸資産　　　　　　　　5,000

解答　　(5)

Chapter 6

6-6

和訳 ABC 社の試算表は次のとおりである。

勘定科目	借方	($) 貸方
現金	9,000	
売掛金	5,600	
棚卸資産	1,000	
建物	18,000	
買掛金		2,500
資本金		15,000
利益剰余金		2,000
売上		30,000
仕入	15,000	
支払利息	900	
	49,500	49,500

決算整理仕訳に必要な情報は以下のとおりである。

① 20X0 年の減価償却費は $2,000 であった。

② 20X0 年 12 月 31 日の棚卸資産勘定残高は $1,200 であった。

修正後残高試算表を完成させなさい。

解答

($)

Account Title	Trial Balance		Adjustment		Adjusted Trial Balance	
	Dr.	Cr.	Dr.	Cr.	Dr.	Cr.
Cash	9,000				9,000	
Accounts receivable	5,600				5,600	
Inventory	1,000		1,200	1,000	1,200	
Building	18,000				18,000	
Accumulated depreciation				2,000		2,000
Accounts payable		2,500				2,500
Share capital		15,000				15,000
Retained earnings		2,000				2,000
Sales		30,000				30,000
Purchases	15,000				15,000	
Interest expense	900				900	
Income summary			1,000	1,200	1,000	1,200
Depreciation expense			2,000		2,000	
Total	49,500	49,500	4,200	4,200	52,700	52,700

6-7

和訳 ABC社は棚卸計算法を使っている。5月1日に、現金€8,000で商品を購入し、6月30日にその商品を€15,000で販売し現金を受け取った。

(a) ABC社は5月1日には、次のどの仕訳を行うべきか。

(1) 現金   8,000

       棚卸資産   8,000

(2) 現金   8,000

       仕入   8,000

(3) 棚卸資産   8,000

       現金   8,000

(4) 棚卸資産   8,000

       仕入   8,000

(5) 仕入   8,000

       現金   8,000

解答：(5)

     ＜参考＞

もし、ABC社がPerpetual inventory system（継続記録法）を使っていれば、解答は(3)となる。

(b) ABC 社は 6 月 30 日には、次のどの仕訳を行うべきか。

(1) 現金   15,000
     売上   15,000

(2) 売上   15,000
     現金   15,000

(3) 現金   15,000
     棚卸資産   8,000
     売上   15,000
     売上原価   8,000

(4) 現金   8,000
     売上原価   8,000
     売上   8,000
     棚卸資産   8,000

(5) 現金   15,000
     売上原価   8,000
     売上   15,000
     棚卸資産   8,000

解答： (1)

＜参考＞

もし、ABC 社が Perpetual inventory system(継続記録法) を使っていれば、解答は (5) となる。

6-8

和訳 会計年度が暦年である ABC 社は、20X0 年度中に次のような取引を行った。

	仕入	売上
3月 3日	$1,000（ 500個×単価$2)	
4月21日		$2,000（ 400個×単価$5)
7月28日	$2,000 (1,000個×単価$2)	
9月10日		$3,000（ 600個×単価$5)
10月 8日	$1,000（ 500個×単価$2)	
11月12日		$4,000（ 800個×単価$5)
12月19日		$ 500（ 100個×単価$5)

期首商品棚卸高は、$200（100 個 × 単価 $2）だった。
ABC 社は、継続記録法を用いている。

(a) 9 月 10 日における以下の金額を計算しなさい。

・売上
・売上原価

(b) 20X0 年度の以下の金額を計算しなさい。

・売上
・売上原価
・棚卸資産

解答

(a) 売上：$3,000
売上原価：600 個 ×$2 = $1,200

(b) 売上：$2,000 + $3,000 + $4,000 + $500 = $9,500
売上原価：(400 個 + 600 個 + 800 個 + 100 個)×$2 = $3,800
棚卸資産：($200 + $1,000 + $2,000 + $1,000) − $3,800 = $400

6-9

和訳 以下の情報は、テキサス社の 20X0 年 3 月における取引に関するものである。

日付	取引内容	数量	単価	合計	数量残高
3/1/20X0	残高	400	$2	$ 800	400
3/7/20X0	仕入	400	4	1,600	800
3/17/20X0	売上	600			200
3/22/20X0	仕入	800	5	4,000	1,000
3/26/20X0	売上	300			700

以下を用いて期末商品棚卸高を計算しなさい。

(1) 先入先出法

(2) 総平均法

(3) 移動平均法

解答 (1) $ 3,500　　(2) $ 2,800　　(3) $ 3,220

解説 (1) $700 \times \$5 = \$3,500$（単価 $2 の期首残高は 3 月 17 日、単価 $4 の 3 月 7 日仕入れ分は 3 月 26 日までに全て販売されて在庫からなくなる。）

(2) 3 月の加重平均単価：$(\$800 + \$1,600 + \$4,000) \div (400 + 400 + 800) = \$4$
期末商品棚卸高：$700 \times \$4 = \$2,800$

(3) 3 月 7 日時点の加重平均単価：$(\$800 + \$1,600) \div 800 = \$3$
3 月 22 日時点の加重平均単価：$(200 \times \$3 + \$4,000) \div 1,000 = \$4.6$
期末商品棚卸高：$700 \times \$4.6 = \$3,220$

Worksheet and Closing Entries

Bookkeeping & Accounting Test for International Communication

BATIC

7-1

和訳　12月31日の支払利息の修正前残高は$15,000であった。すでに支払い義務が発生していて、未払いの利息の金額は$500である。次の仕訳を行いなさい。

(a) 12月31日における未払利息

(b) 支払利息勘定の締切仕訳

解答　(a) Interest expense　　　　　　　500

　　　　　Interest payable　　　　　　　　　　　　500

　　　(b) Income summary　　　　　　15,500

　　　　　Interest expense　　　　　　　　　　　15,500

7-2

和訳 期末の試算表は次のような残高を示していた。(a)収益と(b)費用に関して締切仕訳を行いなさい。

利息収入	$12,000
サービス収入	5,000
給料	5,000
支払利息	500
減価償却費	200
家賃	4,000

解答

(a) Interest income   12,000
     Service income   5,000
         Income summary   17,000

(b) Income summary   9,700
         Salaries expense   5,000
         Interest expense   500
         Depreciation expense   200
         Rent expense   4,000

7-3

和訳 次の T 勘定で示された科目に転記された修正仕訳を行いなさい。

現金	
5,000	

消耗品	
300	150

前払家賃	
2,000	1,000

建物	
50,000	

減価償却累計額	
	5,000

未払利息	
	500

資本金	
	40,000

利益剰余金	
	6,300

サービス収入	
	11,000

支払利息	
500	

家賃	
1,000	

減価償却費	
5,000	

消耗品費	
150	

解答

Interest expense	500	
Interest payable		500
Rent expense	1,000	
Prepaid rent		1,000
Supplies expense	150	
Supplies		150
Depreciation expense	5,000	
Accumulated depreciation		5,000

7-4

和訳 前述の情報に基づいて締切仕訳を行いなさい。

解答

Service income	11,000	
Income summary		11,000
Income summary	6,650	
Interest expense		500
Rent expense		1,000
Depreciation expense		5,000
Supplies expense		150
Income summary	4,350	
Retained earnings		4,350

7-5

和訳 前述 (7-3、7-4) の情報に基づいて締切後試算表を作成しなさい。

解答

Post-Closing Trial Balance

Cash	$ 5,000	
Prepaid rent	1,000	
Supplies	150	
Building	50,000	
Accumulated depreciation		$ 5,000
Interest payable		500
Share capital		40,000
Retained earnings		10,650
	$56,150	$56,150

解説 Retained earnings : $6,300 + $4,350 = $10,650

7-6

和訳 次の情報は 20X0 年 12 月 31 日の ABC 社の勘定に関するものである。

現金	$14,700
受取手形	3,000
建物	20,000
社債	10,000
資本金	7,000
利益剰余金	4,000
売上	30,000
賃借料	1,300
支払給与	12,000

20X0 年 12 月 31 日に終了する年度の当期純利益を求めなさい。

解答 $16,700 ($30,000 − $1,300 − $12,000 = $16,700)

7-7

和訳 前述のケースにおいて、次の締切後試算表を完成させなさい。合計欄以外、金額は借方・貸方のいずれかに記入し、相手方は未記入とすること。

解答

	Dr.	Cr. ($)
Cash	14,700	
Notes receivable	3,000	
Building	20,000	
Bonds payable		10,000
Share capital		7,000
Retained earnings		20,700
Total	37,700	37,700

7-8

和訳 次の勘定に対して締切仕訳を行いなさい。

(a) 売上　　　€50,000

(b) 支払利息　€3,000

(c) 現金　　　€4,000

解答：

(a) Sales　　　　　　　　　　　50,000

　　　Income summary　　　　　　　　50,000

(b) Income summary　　　　　3,000

　　　Interest expense　　　　　　　3,000

(c) 締切仕訳の必要はない。

7-9

和訳 次のステップを適切な順序に並べ替えなさい。

1．元帳へ転記
2．試算表の作成
3．仕訳
4．取引の発生

解答： 4.─3.─1.─2.

7-10

和訳 次の試算表と修正に関する情報から精算表を作成しなさい。

T. ドリュー社
試算表
20X0 年 12 月 31 日

現金	$ 3,500	
売掛金	2,910	
消耗品	1,900	
前払家賃	6,250	
備品	9,000	
買掛金		$ 5,000
支払手形		6,000
資本金		6,000
利益剰余金		2,000
サービス収入		7,500
給料	2,000	
支払利息	600	
一般管理費	340	
	$26,500	$26,500

修正：

(a) 当期の減価償却は $900 であった。

(b) 期末の手元消耗品は $800 であった。

(c) 当期の賃借料は $500 であった。

(d) 未払いの給料は $900 であった。

(e) 未収のサービスは $300 であった。

解答

T. Drew Company
Worksheet
December 31, 20X0

Account Title	Trial Balance Dr.	Trial Balance Cr.	Adjustments Dr.	Adjustments Cr.	Income Statement Dr.	Income Statement Cr.	Balance Sheet Dr.	Balance Sheet Cr.
Cash	3,500						3,500	
Accounts Receivable	2,910		(e) 300				3,210	
Supplies	1,900			(b)1,100			800	
Prepaid Rent	6,250			(c) 500			5,750	
Equipment	9,000						9,000	
Accounts Payable		5,000						5,000
Notes Payable		6,000						6,000
Share Capital		6,000						6,000
Retained Earnings		2,000						2,000
Service Income		7,500		(e) 300		7,800		
Salaries Expense	2,000		(d) 900		2,900			
Interest Expense	600				600			
General Expense	340				340			
	26,500	26,500						
Depreciation Expense			(a) 900		900			
Accumulated Depreciation				(a) 900				900
Supplies Expense			(b)1,100		1,100			
Rent Expense			(c) 500		500			
Salaries Payable				(d) 900				900
			3,700	3,700	6,340	7,800	22,260	20,800
Profit					1,460			1,460
					7,800	7,800	22,260	22,260

7-11

和訳　前述の情報から修正仕訳、締切仕訳を行いなさい。

解答

Adjusting Entries

Depreciation Expense	900	
Accumulated Depreciation		900
Supplies Expense	1,100	
Supplies		1,100
Rent Expense	500	
Prepaid Rent		500
Salaries Expense	900	
Salaries Payable		900
Accounts Receivable	300	
Service Income		300

Closing Entries

Service Income	7,800	
Income Summary		7,800
Income Summary	6,340	
Salaries Expense		2,900
Interest Expense		600
General Expense		340
Depreciation Expense		900
Supplies Expense		1,100
Rent Expense		500
Income Summary	1,460	
Retained Earnings		1,460

7-12

和訳 前述の情報 (7-10、7-11) から損益計算書と貸借対照表を作成しなさい。

T. ドリュー社
損益計算書
20X0 年 12 月 31 日に終了する年度

サービス収入
費用：
　給料
　支払利息
　一般管理費
　減価償却費
　消耗品費
　賃借料
費用合計
当期純利益

T. ドリュー社
貸借対照表
20X0 年 12 月 31 日現在

資産の部		負債および資本の部	
流動資産：		負債：	
現金		買掛金	
売掛金		支払手形	
消耗品		給料	
前払家賃		負債合計	
流動資産計		資本：	
固定資産：		資本金	
備品		利益剰余金	
差引：減価償却累計額		資本合計	
資産合計		負債および資本合計	

解答

T. Drew Company
Income Statement
For the Period Ended December 31, 20X0

Service Income		$7,800
Expenses:		
Salaries Expense	$2,900	
Interest Expense	600	
General Expense	340	
Depreciation Expense	900	
Supplies Expense	1,100	
Rent Expense	500	
Total Expenses		6,340
Profit		$1,460

T. Drew Company
Balance Sheet
As of December 31, 20X0

ASSETS			LIABILITIES AND EQUITY	
Current Assets:			Liabilities:	
Cash		$ 3,500	Accounts Payable	$ 5,000
Accounts Receivable		3,210	Notes Payable	6,000
Supplies		800	Salaries Payable	900
Prepaid Rent		5,750	Total Liabilities	11,900
Total Current Assets		13,260	Equity:	
Non-current Assets:			Share Capital	6,000
Equipment	$9,000		Retained Earnings	3,460
Less:Accumulated Dep.	900	8,100	Total Equity	9,460
			Total Liabilities	
Total Assets		$21,360	and Equity	$21,360

7-13

和訳　次のローズ社の試算表と修正に関する情報から精算表を作成しなさい。

ローズ社
試算表
20X0 年 12 月 31 日

現金	$16,000	
売掛金	18,000	
棚卸資産	4,400	
消耗品	660	
前払保険料	900	
備品	17,000	
減価償却累計額		$ 3,000
買掛金		7,860
支払手形		8,800
資本金		10,000
利益剰余金		7,000
売上		47,700
仕入	18,300	
広告宣伝費	4,200	
賃借料	3,600	
雑費	1,300	
	$84,360	$84,360

決算修正：

(a) 20X0 年 12 月 31 日時点の棚卸資産は、$2,700 であった。

(b) 期末の手元消耗品は $400 であった。

(c) 20X0 年の減価償却費は $1,000 であった。

(d) 当期中の保険料は $400 であった。

解答

Rose Company
Worksheet
December 31, 20X0

Account Title	Trial Balance Dr.	Trial Balance Cr.	Adjustments Dr.	Adjustments Cr.	Income Statement Dr.	Income Statement Cr.	Balance Sheet Dr.	Balance Sheet Cr.
Cash	16,000						16,000	
Accounts Receivable	18,000						18,000	
Merchandise Inventory	4,400		(a)2,700	(a)4,400			2,700	
Supplies	660			(b) 260			400	
Prepaid Insurance	900			(d) 400			500	
Equipment	17,000						17,000	
Accumulated Depreciation		3,000		(c)1,000				4,000
Accounts Payable		7,860						7,860
Notes Payable		8,800						8,800
Share Capital		10,000						10,000
Retained Earnings		7,000						7,000
Sales		47,700				47,700		
Purchases	18,300				18,300			
Advertising Expense	4,200				4,200			
Rent Expense	3,600				3,600			
Miscellaneous Expense	1,300				1,300			
	84,360	84,360						
Income Summary			(a)4,400	(a)2,700	4,400	2,700		
Depreciation Expense			(c)1,000		1,000			
Supplies Expense			(b) 260		260			
Insurance Expense			(d) 400		400			
			8,760	8,760	33,460	50,400	54,600	37,660
Profit					16,940			16,940
					50,400	50,400	54,600	54,600

7-14

和訳 会計サイクルについて、次の記述のうち正しいものはどれか。

(1) 財務諸表の作成後、決算修正仕訳を行うために損益勘定が設けられる。

(2) 試算表は、会計情報を最初に記録する表である。

(3) 転記後の貸借が数学的に一致していることを証明するために、決算修正仕訳が行われる。

(4) 締切仕訳を通じて、収益勘定と費用勘定の残高はゼロになる。

(5) 元帳から仕訳帳へ情報を移転する手続きを転記という。

解答：(4)

Financial Statements

Bookkeeping & Accounting Test for International Communication

BATIC

8-1

和訳 次の項目は、会計期末におけるABC社のものである。

売上	$220,000
仕入返品	300
期首商品棚卸高	50,000
期末商品棚卸高	45,000
仕入運賃	3,000
仕入	198,000

(a)から(c)をそれぞれ計算しなさい。

(a) 純仕入

(b) 売上原価

(c) 売上総利益

解答
(a) Net Purchases $200,700

(b) Cost of Sales $205,700

(c) Gross Profit $ 14,300

8-2

和訳　次の情報を使用して損益計算書を作成しなさい。

手数料収入	$4,000
広告宣伝費	600
給料	1,200
賃借料	780

解答

Income Statement

Fees Income		$4,000
Expenses:		
Advertising Expense	$ 600	
Salaries Expense	1,200	
Rent Expense	780	
Total Expenses		2,580
Profit		$1,420

8-3

和訳　次の情報にもとづき、損益計算書を作成しなさい。

サービス収入	€15,000
保険料	3,000
賃借料	1,500
給料	1,000

解答

Income Statement

Service Income		€15,000
Expenses:		
Insurance Expense	€3,000	
Rent Expense	1,500	
Salaries Expense	1,000	
Total Expenses		5,500
Profit		€ 9,500

Chapter 8

8-4

和訳 次の科目のうち流動資産に分類されるのはどれか。

(1) 備品

(2) 棚卸資産

(3) 土地

(4) 支払手形

(5) 上記のいずれでもない

解答 (2)

8-5

和訳 次の科目のうち固定資産に分類されるのはどれか。

(1) 現金

(2) 買掛金

(3) 資本金

(4) 土地

(5) 上記のいずれでもない

解答 (4)

8-6

和訳 次の科目のうち流動負債に分類されるのはどれか。

(1) 前払家賃

(2) 未払給与

(3) 売掛金

(4) 給料

(5) 上記のいずれでもない

解答 (2)

8-7

和訳 次の科目のうち固定負債に分類されるのはどれか。

(1) 社債

(2) 買掛金

(3) 売掛金

(4) 土地

(5) 上記のいずれでもない

解答 (1)

8-8

和訳 次の資産・負債・資本にもとづいてSSS社の20X0年12月31日の分類された貸借対照表を作成しなさい。

現金	€6,700
買掛金	7,000
車両	1,600
売掛金	800
備品	5,800
資本	7,900

解答

SSS Company
Balance Sheet
As of December 31, 20X0

Assets

Current Assets		
Cash	€ 6,700	
Accounts Receivable	800	
Total Current Assets		€ 7,500
Non-current Assets		
Equipment	5,800	
Vehicles	1,600	
Total Non-current Assets		7,400
Total Assets		€14,900

Liabilities and Equity

Current Liabilities		
Accounts Payable	€ 7,000	
Total Liabilities		€ 7,000
Equity		7,900
Total Liabilities and Equity		€14,900

8-9

和訳　次の情報に基づき、純売上、売上総利益、営業利益を計算しなさい。

売上	$30,000
売上返品	1,300
売上割引	200
売上原価	8,000
営業費用	5,000

解答&解説

Net sales = $30,000 − $1,300 − $200= $28,500

Gross profit = $28,500 − $8,000 = $20,500

Operating profit = $20,500 − $5,000 = $15,500

8-10

和訳　次の情報に基づき、売上原価を計算しなさい。

仕入	$10,000
仕入返品	800
仕入割引	100
仕入運賃	1,200
期首商品棚卸高	1,500
期末商品棚卸高	1,800

解答&解説

Net purchases = $10,000 − $800 − $100 + $1,200 = $10,300

したがって、Cost of sales = $10,300 + $1,500 − $1,800 = $10,000

Chapter 8

8-11

和訳　次の情報はABC社の20X0年12月31日の勘定に関するものである。

勘定科目	金額
現金	$ 7,000
売掛金	5,500
棚卸資産	4,000
土地	20,000
借入金	4,000
資本金	4,500
利益剰余金	3,000
売上	68,000
仕入	35,000
給料	8,000

修正仕訳のための追加情報は以下のとおりである。

・20X0年12月31日の棚卸資産在庫は$4,300である。

・ABC社は20X0年10月1日に$4,000を銀行から借りた。20X0年12月31日に終了する年度に支払利息$70を計上する必要がある。

ABC社の20X0年12月31日に終了する年度の損益計算書を作成しなさい。下記のリストから適切な勘定科目や説明を選びなさい。

1. 仕入	2. 土地	3. 売上原価	4. 当期純利益	5. 支払利息
6. 売上総利益	7. 利益剰余金	8. 未払利息	9. 棚卸資産	

ABC 社
損益計算書
20X0 年 12 月 31 日に終了する年度

売上 $ [   ]
[   ] [   ]
[   ] [   ]

給料 [   ]
[   ] [   ]
[   ] $ [   ]

解答

ABC Company
Income Statement
For the Year Ended December 31, 20X0

Sales $ [68,000]
3. Cost of sales [34,700]
6. Gross profit [33,300]

Salaries expense [8,000]
5. Interest expense [70]
4. Profit $ [25,230]

8-12

和訳 前述のケースにおいて、ABC 社の 20X0 年 12 月 31 日現在の貸借対照表を作成しなさい。下記のリストから適切な勘定科目や説明を選びなさい。

1. 仕入	2. 土地	3. 売上原価	4. 当期純利益	5. 支払利息
6. 売上総利益	7. 利益剰余金	8. 未払利息	9. 棚卸資産	

ABC 社
貸借対照表
20X0 年 12 月 31 日現在

資産		負債及び資本	
現金	$ 7,000	借入金	$ [ ]
売掛金	5,500		[ ]
	[ ]	負債合計	[ ]
	[ ]	資本金	4,500
		利益剰余金	[ ]
		資本合計	[ ]
資産合計	$ [ ]	負債及び資本合計	$ [ ]

解答

ABC Company
Balance Sheet
As of December 31, 20X0

Assets		Liabilities and Equity	
Cash	$ 7,000	Loans payable	$ [4,000]
Accounts receivable	5,500	8. Interest payable	[70]
9. Inventory	[4,300]	Total liabilities	[4,070]
2. Land	[20,000]	Share capital	4,500
		Retained earnings	[28,230]
		Total equity	[32,730]
		Total liabilities and	
Total assets	$ [36,800]	equity	$ [36,800]

8-13

和訳 適切な勘定科目及び(あるいは)記述を記入しなさい。

```
                    ABC 社
                   損益計算書
        20X0 年 12 月 31 日に終了する年度

純売上高                           $45,990
売上原価                            23,300
┌─────────────┐
│      (1)       │                  22,690
└─────────────┘

販売費及び一般管理費                  9,083
┌─────────────┐
│      (2)       │                  13,607
└─────────────┘

支払利息                             5,990
税引前利益                           7,617
法人税                              3,045
┌─────────────┐
│      (3)       │               $  4,572
└─────────────┘
```

解答： (1) Gross profit

(2) Operating profit

(3) Profit

8-14

和訳 適切な勘定科目及び（あるいは）記述を下から選びなさい。

ABC 社
貸借対照表
20X0 年 12 月 31 日現在

資産		負債及び資本	
流動資産：		流動負債：	
現金	$ 2,360	____(3)____	$ 4,290
短期投資	2,400	未払給与	703
売掛金	500	未払法人税	520
____(1)____	460	流動負債合計	5,513
前払利息	520		
流動資産合計	6,240	固定負債：	
		____(4)____	640
固定資産：			
____(2)____	15,000	負債合計	6,153
減価償却累計額	(3,120)		
固定資産合計	11,880	資本：	
		資本金	4,000
		____(5)____	7,967
		資本合計	11,967
資産合計	$18,120	負債及び資本合計	$18,120

設備、利益剰余金、社債、棚卸資産、買掛金

解答：(1) Inventory

(2) Equipment

(3) Accounts payable

(4) Bonds payable

(5) Retained earnings

8-15

和訳　ABC 社は 20X0 年 12 月 31 日に終了する年度に $17,000 の利益を記録した。税率は 25% である。ABC 社は 20X0 年 12 月 31 日に終了する年度に、いくらの法人税費用を認識すべきか。

解答　$4,250

解説　$17,000×25%=$4,250

8-16

和訳　XYZ 社は 20X0 年 12 月 31 日に終了する年度に $35,000 の利益を記録した。税率は 30% である。20X0 年 12 月 31 日に終了する年度に法人税費用を認識する次の仕訳を完成させなさい。

解答

Income tax expense	[10,500]	
Income tax payable		[10,500]

解説　金額は $35,000×30%=$10,500

8-17

和訳　ABC 社は 20X4 年 12 月 31 日に $10,000 の利益剰余金があり、20X5 年中には $3,300 の当期純利益があった。20X5 年 12 月 31 日現在の貸借対照表において、報告すべき利益剰余金はいくらか。

解答＆解説

$10,000 + $3,300 = $13,300

8-18

和訳　前述のケースで、ＡＢＣ社は20X6年中に$1,700の当期純損失があった。20X6年12月31日現在の貸借対照表において、報告すべき利益剰余金はいくらか。

解答＆解説

$13,300 − $1,700 = $11,600

8-19

和訳　ABC 社は $5,000 の現金配当を承認した。次のどの仕訳を行うべきか。

(1)　配当費用　　　　　　　　5,000
　　　　現金　　　　　　　　　　　5,000

(2)　配当費用　　　　　　　　5,000
　　　　未払配当金　　　　　　　　5,000

(3)　利益剰余金　　　　　　　5,000
　　　　現金　　　　　　　　　　　5,000

(4)　利益剰余金　　　　　　　5,000
　　　　未払配当金　　　　　　　　5,000

(5)　仕訳は必要ない。

解答　(4)

8-20

和訳　20X5年12月31日にABC社は €10,000の現金配当を承認し、20X6年1月20日に配当を支払った。20X6年1月20日の仕訳を行いなさい。

解答　Dividends payable　　　　10,000
　　　　　　Cash　　　　　　　　　　　10,000

Basic Assumptions and GAAP

Bookkeeping & Accounting Test for International Communication

BATIC

9-1

和訳　経理担当者が取引の記録や財務諸表の作成をする際に、遵守すべき規準、慣習、ルールを（　　　　　　　　）という。

解答　GAAP または Generally accepted accounting principles（一般に公正妥当を認められた会計原則）

9-2

和訳　費用は賃金が支払われた時点ではなく、サービスが実際に収益に貢献した時点で認識されるという実務を最も適当に正当化しているのは以下のいずれの前提、原則または制約か。
(1) 費用収益対応の原則
(2) 収益認識の原則
(3) 保守主義
(4) 取得原価の原則
(5) 上記のいずれでもない

解答　(1)

9-3

和訳 会社は予見できる将来にわたって事業を続けるという仮定を表しているのは、次のうちどれか。
(1) 企業実体の公準
(2) 会計期間の公準
(3) 継続企業の公準
(4) 貨幣的評価の公準
(5) 上記のいずれでもない

解答 (3)

9-4

和訳 GAAP とは何を表しているか。
(1) 一般に公正妥当と認められた会計原則
(2) 一般に公正妥当と予想された会計原則
(3) 国際的に公正妥当と認められた会計原則
(4) 国際的に公正妥当と予想された会計原則
(5) 上記のいずれでもない

解答 (1)

9-5

和訳 国際財務報告基準（IFRS）を設定しているのは

(1) FASB（Financial Accounting Standards Board, 財務会計基準審議会）

(2) IAS（International Accounting Standards, 国際会計基準）

(3) IASB（International Accounting Standards Board, 国際会計基準審議会）

(4) IOSCO（International Organization of Securities Commission, 証券監督者国際機構）

(5) SEC（Securities and Exchange Commission, 証券取引委員会）

解答 (3)

Financial Statement Analysis

Bookkeeping & Accounting Test for International Communication

BATIC

10-1

和訳 どちらが、より収益性が高い会社か。

	A社	B社
当期純利益率	5%	8%

解答 Company B

10-2

和訳 次の情報に基づき、在庫回転率を計算しなさい。

売上原価	$46,000
棚卸資産	2,000

解答 23

解説 $\dfrac{\$46,000}{\$\ 2,000} = 23$

10-3

和訳 次の情報に基づき、当座比率を計算しなさい。

流動資産	$6,000
棚卸資産	1,000
流動負債	4,000

解答 125%

解説 $\dfrac{\$6,000 - \$1,000}{\$4,000} = 1.25 = 125\%$

10-4

和訳 どちらの会社が、短期負債の返済能力が高いか。

	A 社	B 社
流動資産	$45,000	$70,000
流動負債	$40,000	$50,000

解答 Company B

解説 A 社の流動比率 $\dfrac{\$45,000}{\$40,000} = 1.125 = 112.5\%$

B 社の流動比率 $\dfrac{\$70,000}{\$50,000} = 1.4 = 140\%$

10-5

和訳 この会社の財務構造は債権者にとって改善したか、それとも悪化したか。

	20X0	20X1
負債	$5,500	$7,000
資本	$6,000	$8,000

解答 Improved

解説 20X0 年の負債比率 $\dfrac{\$5,500}{\$5,500 + \$6,000} = 47.8\%$

20X1 年の負債比率 $\dfrac{\$7,000}{\$7,000 + \$8,000} = 46.7\%$

負債比率が下がっているので、長期負債の返済能力は改善したと言える。

10-6

和訳　株主の視点から、どちらの会社が良いか。

	A社	B社
当期純利益	$1,000	$ 4,000
資本	$5,000	$50,000

解答　Company A

解説　A 社の ROE $\dfrac{\$1,000}{\$5,000} = 20\%$

B 社の ROE $\dfrac{\$4,000}{\$50,000} = 8\%$

A社のROEの方が高いので、株主にとっては、A社のほうが良い会社である。

10-7

和訳　次のうちどれが ROA を表しているか。

(1) 資産÷利益

(2) 資産−利益

(3) 資産×利益

(4) 利益÷資産

(5) 利益−資産

解答　(4)

10-8

和訳 以下はカンテ社の財務諸表から抽出されたデータである。

売上	€ 40,000
売上原価	22,000
利益	3,000
総資産	32,000
総負債	7,000
資本	25,000

上記のデータに基づいて、以下の比率を計算しなさい。

(a) 当期純利益率
(b) 株主資本利益率
(c) 総資産回転率

解答 (a) 7.5%

(b) 12.0%

(c) 1.25 回転

Internal Control

Bookkeeping & Accounting Test for International Communication

BATIC

11-1

和訳 内部統制は次のどの目的を達成するために役立つか。

(1) 財務報告の信頼性

(2) 業務の有効性

(3) 法律の遵守

(4) 業務の効率性

(5) 上記すべて

解答 (5)

11-2

和訳 内部統制に関して、次のうち不適当なものを選びなさい。

(1) 現金を取り扱う人をできる限り制限することは良いことだ。

(2) 帳簿をつけることと資産を管理する機能を区分することは良いことだ。

(3) 業務分担を明確にしておくことは当然だ。

(4) 不正を防ぐため、発注、受け取り、及び支払機能は分けておくべきである。

(5) 予算を達成するためには、売上増を図らねばならない。

解答 (5)

11-3

和訳 1月1日、ABC社は$100の定額小口現金を設定した。
この取引を仕訳しなさい。

解答
Petty cash	100	
Cash		100

11-4

和訳 1月中、ABC社は事務用消耗品の購入$12、交通費$28、運賃$32、寄付$8、その他雑費$8を小口現金金庫から支払った。月末時点で小口現金金庫には$12残っていた。この取引の仕訳をしなさい。

解答

Office supplies	12	
Transportation	28	
Freight	32	
Charity	8	
Miscellaneous expense	8	
Cash		88

解説 ABC社は、定額小口現金前渡金制度を採用しており、小口現金前渡金額は$100である。

11-5

和訳 定額小口現金前渡制度は、次の目的で設置される。

(1) 資産の購入
(2) 現金受け取り
(3) 利息の受け取りと支払い
(4) 売上取引
(5) 小額の支払い

解答 (5)

11-6

和訳 20X0年6月30日付の銀行残高調整表を作成するにあたって、ディーン社は以下の情報を明らかにした。

20X0年6月30日時点での当座勘定照合表残高	$3,500
20X0年6月30日時点での帳簿残高	2,730
20X0年6月30日時点での未決済小切手	800
20X0年6月30日時点での未達預金	300
未記帳の6月分銀行サービス手数料	15
未記帳の受取手形銀行回収分	240

さらにディーン社は、簿記係が誤って、6月12日の$249の出金を$294と記帳したことを発見した。

20X0年6月30日時点でのディーン社の正しい現金残高は、

(1) $2,230

(2) $2,455

(3) $3,000

(4) $3,225

(5) 上記のいずれでもない

解答 (3)

解説 20X0年6月30日時点のディーン社の正しい現金残高を求めるためには、当座勘定照合表から求める方法と会社の帳簿残高から求める2つの方法がある。当座勘定照合表から求めるためには、当座勘定照合表上の残高に、調整項目である未決済小切手分と未達預金分のそれぞれの金額を加減算する。この際、未記帳の銀行サービス手数料と受取手形の銀行回収分および出金の記帳ミスは、当座勘定照合表ではなく、会社の帳簿上の調整項目であることに注意する必要がある。よって、当座勘定照合表の残高から求められる正しい現金残高は、$3,500 － $800 ＋ $300 で $3,000 となる。一方、会社の帳簿上の残高から求めると、上記の調整項目により、$2,730 － $15 ＋ $240 ＋ $45で、$3,000 となる。

Accounting for Assets
and Liabilities

Bookkeeping & Accounting Test for International Communication

BATIC

12-1

和訳 20X4年1月1日、ジャクソン社は、業務上必要になったため機械を $72,000で購入した。購入代価に加えて、この機械に関して20X4年に以下の費用が発生した。

購入時の輸送費	$3,600
意図した使用の場所に機械を運んで据え付けるためにかかった費用	2,900
意図した使用が可能な状態になるまでの間に行った、機械が正常に働くかどうかのテストにかかった費用	4,400
意図した使用が可能な状態になった後に行った、機械が正常に働くかどうかのテストにかかった費用	2,700
日常的な機械の維持費用	1,500

ジャクソン社は、この機械の取得原価をいくらで記帳すべきか。

(1) $75,600

(2) $82,900

(3) $84,400

(4) $85,600

(5) $87,100

解答 (2)

解説 有形固定資産の取得原価に算入するのは、その資産を稼働可能にするために必要な場所と状態に置くことに直接起因するコストである。また、保守や修繕に関わる日常的なコストは取得原価に含めない。よって、この機械の取得原価は $82,900（$72,000 + $3,600 + $2,900 + $4,400 = $82,900）となる。

12-2

和訳 20X0年11月1日に、ABC社は古い設備をXYZ社に$100,000で売却した。設備の取得価額は$150,000で、残存価額は$15,000であった。20X0年11月1日現在の減価償却累計額は$54,000だった。ABCは売却損益をいくら認識すべきか。

(1) $(19,000)

(2) $ 0

(3) $ 4,000

(4) $ 11,000

(5) $ 100,000

解答 (3)

解説

Cash	100,000	
Accumulated depreciation	54,000	
Equipment		150,000
Gain on sale		4,000 （差額）

12-3

和訳 BBB 社は次の普通社債を発行した。

発行日	20X1 年 1 月 1 日
満期日	20X4 年 12 月 31 日
額面価額	$ 80,000
表面金利	4%
実効金利	5%
利息の支払い	年に一回 12 月 31 日

次の金額を計算せよ。必要があれば、各金額の小数点以下を四捨五入せよ。

(1) 発行価額

(2) 20X1 年 12 月 31 日に終了する年度の支払利息

(3) 20X1 年 12 月 31 日現在の社債のディスカウント

解答 (1) $77,163

(2) $ 3,858

(3) $ 2,179

解説 (1) 額面価額の現在価値：$80,000 ÷ $(1+5\%)^4$ ≒ $65,816

利息の総支払額の現在価値：$80,000 × 4% ÷ (1+5%) + $80,000 × 4% ÷ $(1+5\%)^2$ + $80,000 × 4% ÷ $(1+5\%)^3$ + $80,000 × 4% ÷ $(1+5\%)^4$ ≒ $11,347

発行価額：$65,816 + $11,347 = $77,163

(2) $77,163 × 5% = $3,858

(3) 20X1年1月1日時点の未償却のディスカウント：$80,000 − $77,163 = $2,837

20X1年12月31日に終了する年度のディスカウント償却額：

$77,163 × 5% − $3,200 ≒ $658

20X1年12月31日時点の未償却のディスカウント：$2,837 − $658 = $2,179

総合練習問題

Bookkeeping & Accounting Test for International Communication

BATIC

1

和訳 次の空欄を埋める最も適切な番号を選びなさい。

お金を借りている立場の人を、 ☐☐☐☐☐☐☐☐☐☐ という。

① 債権者

② 債務者

③ 預金者

④ 雇用者

⑤ 株主

解答 ②

2

和訳 ABC社の資本は$80,000、資産は$93,000である。ABC社の負債はいくらか。

① $0

② $ 13,000

③ $ 40,000

④ $ 86,000

⑤ $173,000

解答 ②

3

和訳 ブラック氏は現金 $25,000 を出資し、XYZ 社を創設した。同時に XYZ 社は同額の普通株式を発行した。その後、XYZ 社は $15,000 の設備を現金で購入した。XYZ 社の資産はいくらか。

① $10,000

② $15,000

③ $25,000

④ $30,000

⑤ $40,000

解答 ③

4

和訳 ABC 社は9月1日に設備€80,000を取得し、€10,000を現金で支払った。残額は9月30日に支払った。ABC 社が9月1日に行うべき仕訳は次のうちどれか。

①設備　　　　80,000
　　　現金　　　　　　10,000
　　　未払金　　　　　70,000

②現金　　　　10,000
　未払金　　　70,000
　　　設備　　　　　　80,000

③設備　　　　80,000
　　　未払金　　　　　80,000

④未払金　　　70,000
　　　現金　　　　　　70,000

⑤現金　　　　70,000
　　　未払金　　　　　70,000

解答 ①

5

和訳 ABC 社は銀行から $50,000 を借りた。次のどの仕訳を行うべきか。

① 現金　　　　50,000
　　　借入金　　　　　　50,000

② 借入金　　　50,000
　　　現金　　　　　　　50,000

③ 現金　　　　50,000
　　　未払金　　　　　　50,000

④ 未払金　　　50,000
　　　現金　　　　　　　50,000

⑤ 借入金　　　50,000
　　　未払金　　　　　　50,000

解答　①

6

和訳

給料		現金	
1,000			1,000

上記取引を適切に表しているのは次のうちどれか。

① 商品を購入した。
② 費用を支払った。
③ 消耗品を購入した。
④ 現金を受け取った。
⑤ 商品を販売した。

解答　②

問題 7 及び 8 は次に基づく。

ABC 社は €700 の商品を XYZ 社に現金で販売した。

7

和訳 ABC 社は次のどの仕訳を行うべきか。

①売上　　　　　　700

　　　現金　　　　　　　700

②売上　　　　　　700

　　　売掛金　　　　　　700

③現金　　　　　　700

　　　売上　　　　　　　700

④売掛金　　　　　700

　　　売上　　　　　　　700

⑤現金　　　　　　700

　　　売掛金　　　　　　700

解答　③

8

和訳 XYZ社は次のどの仕訳を行うべきか。

① 買掛金　　　　700
　　　仕入　　　　　　　700

② 買掛金　　　　700
　　　現金　　　　　　　700

③ 現金　　　　　700
　　　仕入　　　　　　　700

④ 仕入　　　　　700
　　　買掛金　　　　　　700

⑤ 仕入　　　　　700
　　　現金　　　　　　　700

解答 ⑤

9

和訳 XYZ社は$10,000、45日後支払いの利子付手形を額面発行した。金利は12%だった。決済時に、次のどの仕訳を行うべきか。1年を360日と仮定しなさい。

①現金　　　　　10,150
　　支払手形　　　　　　10,000
　　支払利息　　　　　　　　150

②現金　　　　　11,200
　　支払手形　　　　　　10,000
　　支払利息　　　　　　1,200

③支払手形　　　10,000
　　現金　　　　　　　　10,000

④支払手形　　　10,000
　支払利息　　　　150
　　現金　　　　　　　　10,150

⑤支払手形　　　10,000
　支払利息　　　1,200
　　現金　　　　　　　　11,200

解答　④

和訳　ABC社は11月1日に$6,000の商品をXYZ社に30日以内5％割引の条件で販売した。XYZ社が11月20日に支払うとすれば、いくらABC社に支払うべきか。

① $5,700

② $5,800

③ $5,975

④ $5,983

⑤ $6,000

解答　①

解説　期限内なので $300（$6,000×5％ = $300）の Discount が受けられる。

問題 11 及び 12 は次に基づく。

XYZ社は8月1日に現金€20,000で商品を販売した。顧客から破損している部分があるとの苦情が入ったので、現金€900を9月20日に返金した。

11

和訳 XYZ社は8月1日には次のどの仕訳を行うべきか。

① 売掛金　　　　　19,100

　　　　売上　　　　　　　　　19,100

② 売掛金　　　　　20,000

　　　　売上　　　　　　　　　20,000

③ 現金　　　　　　19,100

　　　　売上　　　　　　　　　19,100

④ 現金　　　　　　20,000

　　　　売上　　　　　　　　　20,000

⑤ 現金　　　　　　19,100

　売上返品　　　　　900

　　　　売上　　　　　　　　　20,000

解答　④

和訳　XYZ 社は 9 月 20 日には次のどの仕訳を行うべきか。

①現金　　　　　19,100

　　　売上　　　　　　　19,100

②売上　　　　　　900

　　　売上返品　　　　　　900

③売上返品　　　　900

　　　現金　　　　　　　　900

④売上返品　　　　900

　　　売上　　　　　　　　900

⑤ 仕訳の必要はない。

解答　③

13

和訳 ABC社は11月5日に商品$2,000を掛けで販売した。11月21日に売掛金の決済として、約束手形を受け取った。

11月21日にABC社は、次のどの仕訳を行うべきか。

①売掛金　　　　2,000
　　受取手形　　　　　　2,000
②売掛金　　　　2,000
　　売上　　　　　　　　2,000
③現金　　　　　2,000
　　売掛金　　　　　　　2,000
④受取手形　　　2,000
　　売掛金　　　　　　　2,000
⑤売上　　　　　2,000
　　売掛金　　　　　　　2,000

解答　④

14

和訳

未収利息		受取利息	
1,000			1,000

上記取引を適切に表しているのは次のうちどれか。

① 未収の収益を計上した。

② 未払いの費用を計上した。

③ 利息を受け取った。

④ 現金を受け取った。

⑤ 利息を支払った。

解答　①

15

和訳　利益剰余金　　　52,000

　　　　未払配当金　　　　52,000

上記仕訳を適切に表しているのは次のうちどれか。

① 配当を承認した。

② 配当を払い戻した。

③ 配当を受け取った。

④ 配当を返した。

⑤ 配当を支払った。

解答　①

16

和訳 ABC社は20X4年12月31日に利益剰余金$6,000があり、20X5年中には$800の当期純損失があった。20X5年12月31日現在の貸借対照表において、報告すべき利益剰余金はいくらか。

① $ 800

② $5,200

③ $6,000

④ $6,500

⑤ $6,800

解答 ②

17

和訳 会計年度が暦年であるABC社は、20X0年5月1日に、1年間の火災保険証書を購入し、$1,200を支払った。20X0年12月31日に終了する年度にいくらの支払保険料を報告すべきか。

① $0

② $ 400

③ $ 600

④ $ 800

⑤ $1,200

解答 ④

解説 $1,200 × 8ヵ月/12ヵ月 = $800

18

和訳 会計年度が暦年であるXYZ社は、20X0年9月1日に$8,000で設備を取得した。XYZ社は、定額法で減価償却を行っており、設備は、耐用年数5年、残存価額$2,000と見積もられた。20X0年12月31日に終了する年度に、XYZ社は減価償却費をいくら記録すべきか。

① $0

② $ 400

③ $ 533

④ $1,200

⑤ $1,600

解答 ②

解説 ($8,000 − $2,000)× 4 ヵ月/60 ヵ月 = $400

19

和訳 会計年度が暦年であるABC社は20X0年12月1日に年利8%で€72,000の借入を行った。利息は1年後の満期時に支払うことになっている。20X0年12月31日に次のどの仕訳を行うべきか。1年を360日と仮定しなさい。

①現金　　　　　　　480

　　支払利息　　　　　　　　480

②支払利息　　　　5,760

　　現金　　　　　　　　　5,760

③支払利息　　　　　480

　　未払利息　　　　　　　480

④支払利息　　　　5,760

　　未払利息　　　　　　　5,760

⑤ 仕訳は必要ない。

解答　③

解説　利息の計算　€72,000×8%×30日/360日＝€480

問題 20 及び 21 は次に基づく。

ABC社は棚卸計算法を使っている。5月1日に、商品 \$300 を掛けで購入し、6月30日にその商品を \$700 で販売し現金を受け取った。

20

和訳　ABC 社は 5 月 1 日には、次のどの仕訳を行うべきか。

①棚卸資産	300	
買掛金		300
②棚卸資産	300	
現金		300
③棚卸資産	300	
仕入		300
④仕入	300	
買掛金		300
⑤仕入	300	
現金		300

解答　④

21

和訳 ABC 社は 6 月 30 日には、次のどの仕訳を行うべきか。

①現金　　　　　700
　　　売上　　　　　　　700

②売上　　　　　700
　　　現金　　　　　　　700

③現金　　　　　700
　棚卸資産　　　300
　　　売上　　　　　　　700
　　　売上原価　　　　　300

④現金　　　　　700
　売上原価　　　700
　　　売上　　　　　　　700
　　　棚卸資産　　　　　700

⑤現金　　　　　700
　売上原価　　　300
　　　売上　　　　　　　700
　　　棚卸資産　　　　　300

解答　①

22

和訳　次の情報に基づき、売上原価を計算しなさい。

仕入	$65,000
期首棚卸資産	4,000
期末棚卸資産	2,800
仕入運賃	8,700
仕入返品	1,500

① $65,000

② $71,000

③ $72,200

④ $73,400

⑤ $90,800

解答　④

解説　Net purchases = $65,000 + $8,700 − $1,500 = $72,200

Cost of sales = $72,200 + $4,000 − $2,800 = $73,400

問題 23 及び 24 は次に基づく。

ABC 社の 10 月 31 日の勘定残高と 11 月中の取引は次のとおりであった。

10 月 31 日現在の勘定残高

現金	$10,000
売掛金	3,000

11 月中の取引

11 月 1 日	事務用消耗品に現金 $1,500 を支払った。
2 日	売掛金の決済として現金 $2,000 を受け取った。
2 日	商品を $5,000 で掛けで販売した。
10 日	水道光熱費に現金 $150 を支払った。
13 日	売掛金の決済として現金 $3,000 を受け取った。
18 日	商品を販売し、現金 $4,000 を受け取った。
25 日	商品を $1,000 で掛けで販売した。

23

和訳 11 月 30 日の現金残高はいくらか。

① $ 8,350

② $ 8,500

③ $16,850

④ $17,000

⑤ $17,350

解答 ⑤

解説 $10,000 − $1,500 + $2,000 − $150 + $3,000 + $4,000 = $17,350

24

和訳　11 月 30 日の売掛金残高はいくらか。

① $1,000

② $2,000

③ $3,000

④ $4,000

⑤ $5,000

解答　④

解説　$3,000 − $2,000 + $5,000 − $3,000 + $1,000 = $4,000

25

和訳　買掛金は、次のどの区分に分類されるか。

① 流動資産

② 流動負債

③ 有形固定資産

④ 固定負債

⑤ 資本

解答　②

26

和訳 流動資産に分類されるのは、次のうちどれか。

① 土地

② 買掛金

③ 売掛金

④ 設備

⑤ 資本金

解答 ③

27

和訳 次のステップを適切な順序に並べ替えなさい。

(1) 総勘定元帳への転記

(2) 試算表の作成

(3) 仕訳

(4) 取引の発生

解答 ⑤

和訳　空欄を埋めなさい

修正仕訳が必要なのは、財務諸表が [＿＿＿＿＿＿＿] に基づいて記録され
ているからである。

① 発生主義

② 資産主義

③ 現金主義

④ 資本主義

⑤ 負債主義

解答　①

和訳　内部統制目的のために、原則として企業は、少額の諸経費の支払いに
[＿＿＿＿＿＿＿] を使用する。

上記空欄に最も適切な番号を選びなさい。

① 会計システム

② 定額小口現金前渡制度

③ 棚卸計算法

④ 継続記録法

⑤ 単式簿記

解答　②

30

和訳　モスコン社は、5 月 31 日時点の銀行残高調整表に関して、以下の情報を有していた。

当座預金の帳簿残高	€4,500
不渡小切手	220
未記帳の受取手形の回収	390

5 月 31 日時点におけるモスコン社の正しい当座預金残高を計算しなさい。

解答　€4,670

問題 31 及び 32 は次に基づく。

ABC 社の1月中の取引は次のとおりである。

日付　　　取引

10　　$10,000 の商品を現金で購入した。

20　　売掛金の決済として、現金 $3,000 と手形 $7,000 を受け取った。

30　　商品を掛けで $6,000 で販売した。

31

和訳　適切な番号を下から選び、仕訳を行いなさい。

1/10　Dr. (　　　　　　) 　　10,000

　　　　Cr. (　　　　　　) 　　　　　　10,000

1/20　Dr. (　　　　　) 　　　3,000

　　　　　 (　　　　　) 　　　7,000

　　　　Cr. (　　　　　) 　　　　　　10,000

1/30　Dr. (　　　　　) 　　　6,000

　　　　Cr. (　　　　　) 　　　　　　6,000

1．買掛金	2．仕入返品	3．仕入	4．現金
5．売掛金	6．受取手形	7．売上	8．売上返品

解答　1/10　Dr. (　3　) 　　10,000

　　　　　　 Cr. (　4　) 　　　　　10,000

　　　1/20　Dr. (　4　) 　　3,000

　　　　　　　 (　6　) 　　7,000

　　　　　　 Cr. (　5　) 　　　　　10,000

　　　1/30　Dr. (　5　) 　　6,000

　　　　　　 Cr. (　7　) 　　　　　6,000

32

和訳 取引を下記の T 勘定に記入しなさい。勘定科目については、適切な番号を
下記リストより選びなさい。勘定科目と金額のみを記入すること。

1．買掛金	2．仕入返品	3．仕入	4．現金
5．売掛金	6．受取手形	7．売上	8．売上返品

解答：

	3				4	
10,000				3,000		10,000

	5				6	
6,000		10,000		7,000		

	7	
		6,000

33

和訳 XYZ 社は次の取引があった。

8月20日	XYZ 社は $400 の商品を販売者に返品した。商品は以前掛けで購入されたものだった。

仕訳帳に記入し、元帳に転記しなさい。適切な勘定名、参照、金額を記入しなさい。元帳勘定の「説明」欄と「残高」欄は空欄にすること。

解答

	General Journal			J6
Date	Account and Explanation	P.R.	Dr.	Cr.
Aug. 20	Accounts payable	201	400	
	Purchase returns and allowance	511		400

	Accounts payable				201
Date	Explanation	P.R.	Debit	Credit	Balance
Aug. 20		J6	400		

	Purchase returns and allowance				511
Date	Explanation	P.R.	Debit	Credit	Balance
Aug. 20		J6		400	

34

和訳 ABC 社は次の固定資産を保有していた。

	取得日	取得原価	耐用年数	残存価額	減価償却方法
建物	20X2年1月1日	$120,000	10 年	$10,000	定額法
オフィス設備	20X4年1月1日	$ 6,000	5 年	$ 600	2倍定率法
機械装置	20X5年1月1日	$ 15,000	5 年	$ 1,500	級数法

ABC の会計年度は 12 月 31 日に終了する。

20X5 年の財務諸表において ABC 社が報告すべき次の金額を計算しなさい。

1．建物の減価償却費　　　　　　$ [　　　　]
2．建物の減価償却累計額　　　　$ [　　　　]
3．オフィス設備の減価償却費　　$ [　　　　]
4．機械装置の減価償却費　　　　$ [　　　　]

解答＆解説

1．($120,000 − $10,000) ÷ 10 年 = $11,000

2．$11,000 × 4 年 = $44,000

3．償却率は 1 ÷ 5 年 × 2 = 0.4

20X4 年減価償却費 = $6,000 × 0.4 = $2,400

したがって 20X5 年減価償却費 = ($6,000 − $2,400) × 0.4 = $1,440

4．償却率は 5/(5+4+…+1) = 5/15

したがって減価償却費は ($15,000 − $1,500) × 5/15 = $4,500

和訳 次の情報は ABC 社の 20X0 年 12 月 31 日の勘定に関するものである。

勘定科目	金額
現金	€ 8,000
売掛金	2,000
建物	7,000
買掛金	?
社債	2,000
資本金	4,000
利益剰余金	2,000
売上	30,000
仕入	20,000
費用	2,000

買掛金の金額を計算し、ABC の試算表を作成しなさい。合計欄以外、金額は借方・貸方のいずれかに記入し、相手側は未記入とすること。

解答

ABC Company
Trial Balance
December 31, 20X0

(€)

Account Title	Dr.	Cr.
Cash	8,000	
Accounts receivable	2,000	
Building	7,000	
Accounts payable		1,000
Bonds payable		2,000
Share capital		4,000
Retained earnings		2,000
Sales		30,000
Purchases	20,000	
Expenses	2,000	
Total	39,000	39,000

36

和訳 次の財務データは A 社と B 社の財務諸表から抜き出したものである。

	A 社	B 社
売上	$ 88,000	$54,000
当期純利益	5,000	4,000
流動資産	4,000	4,000
固定資産	109,000	90,000
流動負債	3,000	4,000
固定負債	40,000	10,000
資本	70,000	80,000

必要があれば小数点第 2 位を四捨五入しなさい。

(1) ［　　　］にあてはまる数字を計算し、（　　　）の正しい答えに丸をつけなさい。

A 社の当期純利益率は［　　　］％であり、B 社の当期純利益率は［　　　］％であるから、（　A　　B　）社のほうが収益性が高い。

(2) ［　　　］にあてはまる数字を計算し、（　　　）の正しい答えに丸をつけなさい。

A 社の ROE は［　　　］％であり、B 社の ROE は［　　　］％であるから、（　A　　B　）社のほうが株主にとって良い。

(3) どちらの会社が、短期負債の返済能力が高いか。正しい答えに丸をつけなさい。
A 社　　　　　　B 社

解答　(1) Because Company A's profit margin is [　5.7　] % while Company
　　　　　B's profit margin is [　7.4　] %, Company (A (B)) is more
　　　　　profitable.

　　　(2) Because Company A's ROE is [　7.1　] % while Company B's ROE is
　　　　　[　5　] %, Company ((A) B) is better for shareholders.

　　　(3) (Company A)　　　　　　　Company B

解説　(3) A 社の流動比率 133.3%、B 社の流動比率 100%

問題 37 及び 38 は次に基づく。

次の情報は ABC 社の 20X0 年 12 月 31 日の勘定に関するものである。

勘定科目	金額
現金	$ 7,000
売掛金	4,000
棚卸資産	2,500
事務用消耗品	1,000
土地	11,000
買掛金	4,000
資本金	5,000
利益剰余金	3,000
売上	41,500
仕入	18,000
賃借料	10,000

修正仕訳のための追加情報は次のとおりである。

(1) 20X0 年 12 月 31 日の棚卸資産在庫は $1,200 である。

(2) $1,000 の事務用消耗品は購入時に資産勘定に計上された。20X0 年 12 月 31 日に $400 分が未使用であった。

和訳　ABC社の20X0年12月31日に終了する年度の損益計算書を作成しなさい。下記のリストから適切な勘定科目や説明を選びなさい。

1．売上総利益	2．棚卸資産	3．売上原価	4．仕入
5．事務用消耗品費	6．当期純利益	7．利益剰余金	8．土地

ABC 社
損益計算書
20X0 年 12 月 31 日に終了する年度

売上　　　　　　　　　　　　　　　　$ 41,500

　　　　　　　　　　　　　　　　　　[　　　　]
　　　　　　　　　　　　　　　　　　[　　　　]

賃借料　　　　　　　　　　　　　　　10,000

　　　　　　　　　　　　　　　　　　[　　　　]
　　　　　　　　　　　　　　　　　　$ [　　　　]

解答

ABC Company
Income Statement
For the Year Ended December 31, 20X0

Sales	$ 41,500
3. Cost of sales	[19,300]
1. Gross profit	[22,200]
Rent expense	10,000
5. Office supplies expense	[　600]
6. Profit	$ [11,600]

38

和訳 ABC社の20X0年12月31日現在の貸借対照表を作成しなさい。下記のリストから適切な勘定科目や説明を選びなさい。

1. 売上総利益	2. 棚卸資産	3. 売上原価	4. 仕入
5. 事務用消耗品費	6. 当期純利益	7. 利益剰余金	8. 土地

ABC社
貸借対照表
20X0年12月31日現在

資産			負債及び資本		
現金	$	7,000	買掛金	$	4,000
売掛金		4,000	負債合計		4,000
[ ]	[	]	資本金	[	]
事務用消耗品	[	]	[ ]	[	]
[ ]	[	]	資本合計	[	]
資産合計	$[	]	負債及び資本合計	$[	]

解答

ABC Company
Balance Sheet
As of December 31, 20X0

Assets			Liabilities and Equity		
Cash	$	7,000	Accounts payable	$	4,000
Accounts receivable		4,000	Total liabilities		4,000
2. Inventory	[	1,200]	Share capital	[	5,000]
Office supplies	[	400]	7. Retained earnings	[	14,600]
8. Land	[	11,000]	Total equity	[	19,600]
Total assets	$[	23,600]	Total liabilities and equity	$[	23,600]

〈BATIC企画委員会〉（敬称略・順不同）

委 員 長　　平松　一夫
委　　員　　井上　達男
委　　員　　秋葉　賢一
委　　員　　田宮　治雄
委　　員　　又邊　崇

BATIC（国際会計検定）® 公式問題集

2021年　2月25日　初版第1刷発行
2022年　6月10日　初版第2刷発行

編　　集　東京商工会議所
発 行 者　湊元　良明
発 行 所　東京商工会議所
　　　　　検定センター
　　　　　〒100-0005　東京都千代田区丸の内3-2-2
　　　　　（丸の内二重橋ビル）
　　　　　TEL（03）3989-0777
協　　力　（株）イーストゲート
発 売 元　（株）中央経済グループパブリッシング
　　　　　〒101-0051　東京都千代田区神田神保町1-31-2
　　　　　TEL（03）3293-3381
　　　　　FAX（03）3291-4437
印 刷 所　こだま印刷（株）

©2021　東京商工会議所　Printed in Japan
ISBN978-4-502-38511-7 C3034